QUAALUDES

Maryann Ziemer

—The Drug Library—

Enslow Publishers, Inc.

44 Fadem Road	PO Box 38
Box 699	Aldershot
Springfield, NJ 07081	Hants GU12 6BP
USA	UK

Dedicated to Ed, and to our sons and daughters
Greg, Erica, Jeff, and Andrea.

Publisher's Note

Over time, the term methaqualone has been generally used as quaaludes, as defined in Merriam Webster's Collegiate Dictionary, Tenth Edition. For purposes of this book, we will be referring to the use of methaqualone as quaalude or quaaludes. Any reference in this book to the pills or products manufactured by Willaim H. Rorer, Inc. will be referred to as Quaaludes™.

Library of Congress Cataloging-in-Publication Data

Ziemer, Maryann.
      Quaaludes / Maryann Ziemer.
         p. cm. —(The drug library)
      Includes bibliographical references and index.
      Summary: Examines the history, physical effects, and societal effects of quaaludes.
      ISBN 0-89490-847-2
      1. Methaqualone abuse—Juvenile literature. 2. Methaqualone—Physiological effect—Juvenile literature. [1. Methaqualone. 2. Drug abuse. 3. Drugs.] I. Title. II. Series.
RC568.M45Z53 1997
613.8—dc20   96-13597
                                           CIP
                                           AC

Printed in the United States of America

10 9 8 7 6 5 4 3 2

Photo Credits: Courtesy of *HIGH TIMES* magazine, p. 76; Courtesy of the Lloyd Library & Museum, Cincinnati, Ohio, pp. 7, 8; Courtesy Shriners Hospital for Children, p. 82; Courtesy of the U.S. Drug Enforcement Administration, pp. 31, 42; EMB-Service for Publishers, p. 67; Enslow Publishers, Inc., p. 21; Maryann Ziemer, pp. 24, 47, 92; William H. Helfand Collection, New York, pp. 13, 19, 52, 61.

Cover Photo: "Images © 1995 Photo Disc, Inc."

Contents

1
The History of Quaaludes

Looking back into history, we find that people have been using mind-altering substances for thousands of years. In all parts of the world and in many different civilizations and cultures, people seem to have found something to eat, drink, or inhale that could change how they felt, thought, or behaved.

Early mind-altering substances came from natural sources. Ancient Sumerians, people who lived in a region that is now part of southern Iraq, collected the juice from the opium poppy and cooked it into a gum. They chewed the gum, smoked it, or mixed it with liquids and drank it.

The Incas of South America discovered long ago that chewing coca leaves mixed with ash released the coca plant's active ingredient, cocaine, into their saliva.

Archaeologists, scientists who study the remains of ancient civilizations, found the remains of a Scythian burial ground, well preserved in frozen Siberia and dating from 400 B.C. It contained metal tent poles and copper containers. The remains indicate that inside their tent, the ancient people inhaled the smoke of burning hemp as it rose from the copper containers.[1] Hemp is the plant that marijuana comes from.

The use of mind-altering substances by earlier people was usually approved by members of their society or culture. Sometimes the use was a part of sacred rituals or in celebration of important events. Native Americans in the Lake Superior region of the United States used a potent red-topped mushroom in their ceremonies.[2] In the Southwest, other Native Americans used the mind-altering effects of the peyote cactus in their rituals. Today, museums display fans, rattles, and staffs decorated by Native Americans with fine beading done in the "peyote" stitch.[3]

Sometimes mind-altering substances were used to ease hunger, exhaustion, or pain. There is evidence that people have recognized and valued the medicinal and healing properties of certain substances for a long time. Archaeologists have found objects that tell the story of ancient cultures' use of mind-altering plants and fungi. They found beautifully decorated jars and finely crafted bowls for storage; carved pipes, tubes, and trays for smoking and snuffing; and elegant shallow metal pans, called braziers, for burning plant leaves, roots, and gums. The smoke gave relief to the sick and visions to the shaman, the community member believed to have a connection with the spirit world. Written descriptions from ages past also reveal that users suffered from addictions to their natural mind-altering substances.

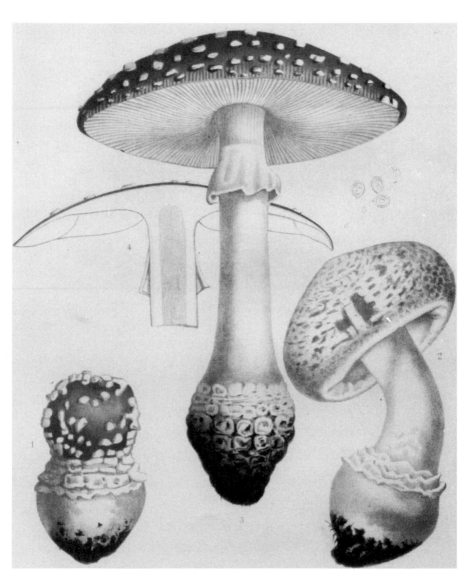

The hallucinogenic mushroom *Amanita muscaria*, also called the "fly-agaric" toadstool, is bright with white dots. Eating the mushroom has caused visions of "fly-agaric men" who have no necks or legs.

The peyote cactus contains the hallucinogenic ingredient mescaline. Eating its mescaline "buttons" produces images of moving light and shadow, kaleidoscopic shapes, and colors. It can also produce nausea and vomiting.

The Modern Age of Chemistry and Synthetic Drugs

In more recent history, the science of chemistry has brought entirely different kinds of mind-altering substances into existence. We know now how to combine chemicals to create new synthetic drugs and medicines. In the ongoing search for safer and more effective drugs, medicines, and anesthetics, research laboratories have created many mind-altering or psychoactive drugs.

We call these drugs psychoactive because they affect the functions of the brain, which control all of our mental, emotional, and physical activity. Some psychoactive drugs stimulate physical and mental activity, some calm and sedate the user. Used appropriately, psychoactive drugs can help people suffering from anxiety or depression. As anesthetics, they can induce the safe, deep sleep necessary for surgery. Used inappropriately, they are addicting and extremely dangerous.

In 1955 in India, a chemical called methaqualone (pronounced meth-ah-quay-lone) was created. It was made in the laboratories of researchers who were trying to develop a drug to fight malaria, a serious worldwide disease transmitted by mosquitoes.

As they tested the chemical for its medicinal properties, the researchers found that methaqualone had sedative and hypnotic effects. As a sedative, it quieted and relaxed people. As a hypnotic, it put them to sleep. Furthermore, unlike other sedative-hypnotics in use at the time, methaqualone appeared not to seriously affect the brain's respiration control center or dream stage of sleep. Researchers thought they had created a safe, therapeutic, and nonaddicting sedative-hypnotic drug.[4]

In 1965, pharmaceutical companies in the United States began to make methaqualone and doctors began to prescribe it for people suffering from anxiety, nervousness, and insomnia. It was sold under trade names such as Sopor™, Parest™, and Optimil™. One of the U.S. manufacturers of methaqualone, William H. Rorer, Inc., called its methaqualone sleeping pills "Quaaludes™." Over time, the term methaqualone has been generally used as quaaludes, as defined in Merriam Webster's Collegiate Dictionary, Tenth Edition. For purposes of this book, we will be referring to the use of methaqualone as quaalude or

9

quaaludes. Any reference in this book to the pills or products manufactured by Willaim H. Rorer, Inc. will be referred to as Quaaludes™.

Quaaludes Become Extremely Popular

At first, quaaludes was not a controlled substance. This meant that the federal government placed no restrictions on their prescribed use. Doctors freely wrote prescriptions for people who complained of stressful days and sleepless nights. Sometimes the prescriptions were simply phoned in to the drugstore. Pharmacists usually filled the prescriptions in two strengths, 150 milligrams and 300 milligrams.

Quaaludes quickly became an extremely popular drug and huge numbers of prescriptions were written. They became so popular because people learned to like the way the pills made them feel—relaxed and tingly, friendly, euphoric, uninhibited. Quaaludes were perceived as pleasantly intoxicating downers, similar to alcohol, and gained the reputation of enhancing sex, of being a "love drug."

Quaaludes were very popular in this country in the 1960s when a spirit of rebellion and an emerging drug culture were sweeping the country. The pills soon became recreational or social drugs. A recreational drug is used not for medical purposes, but for the physical or mental effects it produces which are considered pleasurable. Celebrity musicians, entertainers, and trendsetters openly used many mind-altering drugs, quaaludes prominently among them. High school and college students used quaaludes in social and political gatherings. They called the pills by a number of nicknames, such as "quads," "sopers," and "ludes," taken from pharmaceutical company trade names. Quaaludes were so widely used among young people who camped out during the 1972 national political conventions that Flamingo Park in Miami Beach became known as "Quaalude Alley."[5] The pills were easily available in great numbers on college campuses. Taking "ludes" and "luding out" (combining alcohol and quaaludes) were common practices at universities across the country. Quaaludes had become a chosen drug of abuse.

Even though they were outwardly being prescribed for medical reasons, the demand for quaaludes as a so-called recreational drug made dealing in the drug very profitable. People would sell their legally filled prescriptions on the street. There was also a supply of illegal, counterfeit quaaludes. The "look-alike" ludes were identical in appearance to the legally made tablets and capsules, but they were produced in secret labs with no controls on quality or purity.

Quaaludes Were Found to Be Not So Safe After All

As the use of quaaludes increased and spread, hospital emergency rooms began receiving people with quaalude-related conditions. Some were having seizures and convulsions. Some went into unconscious, comatose states. It was reported that eighty-eight people died from quaalude overdose in the United States in 1974.[6] For all the talk about quaaludes' safe and nonaddicting qualities, there were serious problems with the drug's use.

Quaaludes were found to be strongly addicting. Regular use caused psychological and physical dependence. Users developed

11

tolerance to them, which meant that increasingly large amounts had to be taken to get the desired effect. If users had become physically dependent, attempts to stop quaalude use resulted in severe withdrawal symptoms, so users showed up in emergency rooms. Between May 1976 and April 1977, an estimated fifty-five hundred emergency room visits were related to quaalude use and withdrawal symptoms.[7]

In 1982, in response to the seriousness of quaalude use and abuse in the United States, the federal government reclassified quaaludes. The drug's status changed from an unrestricted prescription drug to a Schedule II drug. This meant that while it was still recognized as having some medical and therapeutic uses, it also had potential for a high rate of abuse. Restrictions were placed on manufacturing, prescribing, and dispensing quaaludes. Pharmaceutical companies could produce only set amounts of the drug, based on the previous year's quota. Every pill had to be strictly accounted for. Doctors had to be registered with the Drug Enforcement Agency in order to write prescriptions for quaaludes, and the prescriptions had to be *written*. They could not be phoned in to the drugstore or pharmacy. They could not be refilled. Pharmacists also had to be registered with the Drug Enforcement Agency in order to fill quaalude prescriptions, and they had to keep multiple records of each prescription. They were required to provide strictly secured storage space for the drug and the prescription forms.

As a Schedule II drug, quaaludes became harder to obtain legally. So various semi-legal schemes were developed for obtaining prescriptions for the drug. One scheme was the "stress clinic." In these clinics, licensed physicians were set up to give quick examinations and brief evaluations to people who came in and

In William Shakespeare's play Romeo and Juliette, Romeo pays the apothecary forty ducats for a dram of poison. Juliette, in the meantime, has visited a monk knowledgeable about psychoactive substances and gotten a drug which will cause her to appear dead but which, in reality, puts her into a very deep, death-like sleep.

complained of stress. The doctors then readily wrote prescriptions for a one-month supply of quaaludes. The prescriptions could easily be filled at pharmacies and drugstores. Many of the pills obtained with "stress clinic" prescriptions were then illegally resold on the street. Even with the cost of a visit to the clinic and the expense of having the prescription filled, people still made a profit on the pills' illegal resale.

"Juice bars" also sprang up. There, people gathered to socialize and take quaaludes, often in combination with juices, or sometimes wine. "Luding out" with wine became a popular but hazardous activity. Both quaaludes and alcohol depress the central nervous system and together they boost each others' effects. Most deaths related to quaaludes were from combinations of quaaludes and alcohol.[8]

In 1984, quaaludes were again reclassified by the federal government, this time to Schedule I, where it joined heroin, marijuana, and other drugs with no approved medical use. As a Schedule I drug, quaaludes became illegal to make (except for specifically approved research purposes), to prescribe, to sell, and to possess. Soon after, all legal production of quaaludes stopped in the United States. Illegal operations did continue, however, and counterfeit quaaludes continued to be smuggled into the country for sale on the streets.

Quaaludes Today

Quaalude use fell off dramatically after 1982. A check of Drug Enforcement Administration records indicates that between 1991 and 1994, an average of about twenty quaalude-related cases were recorded per year. This is far below the average of the

14

preceding decade. Today, those drugs sold on the street as quaaludes are believed to come from Mexico.[9] The ingredients that they actually contain are often unknown. Their strength and purity vary widely and are unreliable. Because of this, using them is quite dangerous.

Although the use of quaaludes has decreased, a new drug of abuse has emerged which threatens to become the quaaludes of the 90s. The drug is Rohypnol™, or "roofies," as it is known on the street.

Rohypnol is a potent, long-lasting sedative. It causes muscles to relax, produces short-term amnesia, or loss of memory, and induces sleep. Before its sedative effect takes over, it lowers inhibitions. Cases of rape, in which unaware women were given Rohypnol and then were sexually assaulted while sedated, have been reported. The women wake up not knowing what has happened to them.[10]

Rohypnol first showed up in the United States in Florida in 1989. It has grown in popularity and is reported to be almost as widely used as LSD and marijuana. In schools and nightclubs, Rohypnol has been added as a drug of choice.

Rohypnol is made by Hoffman-LaRoche, a Swiss pharmaceutical company, and is sold by prescription in many European and South American countries. In some Mexican drugstores, it is available over the counter—that is, without a prescription, much like aspirin or cough medicine.

Rohypnol is not approved for use in the United States and is not made in the United States. The mere possession of Rohypnol is illegal because it is a controlled substance. Possession is punishable by both fines and prison.

Street Names for Quaaludes

Billy Boots	Mandrakes
Disco Biscuits	Pillows
Dr. Jekyll and Mr. Hyde	Q's
French Quaalude	Quacks
Heroin for Lovers	Quads
Lemmon 714's	Soapers, Sopes
Love Drug	Sopers, Sopors
Ludes	Vitamin Q

Rohypnol is often smuggled into Florida, Texas, and other Southern states from Mexico and Colombia. Drug Enforcement Agency officials have seized fifty thousand pills at a time in Texas and Louisiana.[11]

Frequent use of Rohypnol can result in tolerance and addiction. A Miami drug hot line reports receiving calls from teens who had grown dependent on "roofies" and wanted help. When used with alcohol, Rohypnol has the life-threatening effects of quaaludes combined with alcohol. But the effects of Rohypnol taken with alcohol are even greater and much longer lasting than the effects of quaaludes and alcohol. It was a combination of Rohypnol and champagne that caused the breathing depression that put musician Kurt Cobain into a coma one month before his suicide.[12]

"Roofies" have the potential to become the "ludes" of the future. The awareness that resulted from the quaalude experience should be a warning against the abuse of Rohypnol.

Questions for Discussion

1. Anesthetics are psychoactive drugs used in hospitals so that people can have surgery without pain. Discuss how this use differs from the use of a psychoactive street drug like quaaludes.

2. "Recreation" is defined as refreshing the mind or body with a diverting activity. People sometimes refer to nontherapeutic, psychoactive drugs as "recreational" drugs. Discuss the appropriateness of the term "recreational drug."

3. Describe an archaeological dig in your town two thousand years from now. (All has been well preserved.) What conclusions do you think would be drawn about peoples' means of recreation?

2

What Quaaludes Are and What Quaaludes Do

Psychoactive drugs fall into four basic categories. There are stimulants, often called uppers; depressants, often called downers; psychedelics; and inhalants as well as other miscellaneous drugs.

Uppers such as cocaine and amphetamines increase heart rate and breathing. Downers such as heroin, barbiturates, and quaaludes decrease heart rate and breathing. Psychedelics such as LSD and marijuana act by confusing the senses and causing illusions not based in reality. The last category—inhalants and miscellaneous drugs—includes nitrous oxide and volatile (explosive) substances such as gasoline, which produce feelings of intoxication. It also includes other substances, from embalming fluid (formaldehyde) to lighter fluid, which produce an array of psychoactive drug effects.[1]

POPULAR
FRENCH TONIC WINE
Fortifies and Refreshes Body & Brain
Restores Health and Vitality

In the 1800s, an Italian doctor named Mariani had the idea to add coca to wine. The cocaine-containing Vin Mariani was advertised as a cure for sickness and pain and as an energy booster. It was widely used. Dr. Mariani made a fortune.

Quaaludes, whose psychoactive ingredient is the chemical methaqualone, fall into the downer category because the drug acts by depressing the central nervous system—the brain and spinal cord. Breathing, heart rate, and muscle tension are affected. A low dose of quaaludes has sedative effects. It relaxes and calms. Larger doses produce a hypnotic effect, which means that it causes sleep.

Quaaludes' Psychoactive Chemical Ingredient

The psychoactive chemical in quaaludes, methaqualone, is a white, bitter-tasting crystalline powder that dissolves in alcohol, ether, and chloroform. It is very difficult to dissolve it in water. It is stored in body fat and is eliminated from the body slowly. In addition to its sedative-hypnotic properties, methaqualone also has anti-convulsive and cough-suppressing properties.[2]

Methaqualone's chemical name is 2-methyl-3-0-tolyl-4(3H)-quinazolinone. Its structural formula is shown on the following page.[3]

If you count the atoms, you find that methaqualone contains sixteen carbon atoms, fourteen hydrogen atoms, two nitrogen atoms, and one oxygen atom. The drug's line formula is written as $C_{16}H_{14}N_2O$.

To make quaaludes, a process which is now illegal in the United States, the white crystalline methaqualone powder is pressed into tablets or put into capsules. They were originally prescribed to be taken by mouth.

Methaqualone was also available in other countries under names such as Melsedrin™, Tuazolone™, and Mequin™. In

A Methaqualone Molecule

The molecular formula of methaqualone is shown here.

England it was available in combination with an antihistamine under the name Mandrax™.[4] Legitimate production of methaqualone stopped worldwide in 1988, and today there is no legal supplier of methaqualone in the world.

Today quaaludes are produced in illegal, secret locations where poor manufacturing conditions and lack of quality controls often yield contaminated products of unknown content and unpredictable strength. Although they are sold on the streets as quaaludes, some tablets contain no methaqualone at all. Instead, they are composed of a variety of substances, such as large amounts of tranquilizers like Valium™, sometimes the psychedelic PCP, and antihistamines.[5] Fillers, such as sugar, are also used in street drugs that are passed off as quaaludes.

The Brain Is the Center of Control

The brain is the most remarkable organ in our body. It controls all life processes, often without us being the least bit aware of what it is doing. How often and deeply we breathe, how strongly and regularly our heart beats, when digestive fluids need to flow from cells lining our stomach—these are all functions controlled by the brain.

The brain very precisely orders the body's cells to make many different natural chemicals. Some of these biochemicals are found in very small but extremely powerful amounts in nerve cells called neurons.

The brain has 100 billion neurons.[6] The biochemicals in the neurons are called neurotransmitters. They are the means by which all action, thought, feeling, and emotion occur in our body and brain.

22

A neurotransmitter does its work by passing from one neuron to another across a tiny space called a synapse. (See figure on next page.) When a neurotransmitter leaves its neuron, crosses the synapse, and fits into a neighbor neuron, it carries a message. After the message has been transmitted, the neurotransmitter may return to its previous neuron to be used again. It may be changed to some other useful biochemical, or it may be broken apart and eliminated.

Messages that neurotransmitters carry can make us feel good. They are responsible for that tired but pleasantly relaxed feeling we get after working or playing hard, and for the feeling of satisfied fullness we get after we have eaten. The neurotransmitters, under the master direction of our brain, can stimulate, calm, or excite. They can also cause us to feel sad, scared, or depressed.

Of all the organs in our body, the brain is the most well protected. It is enclosed in a thick, heavy skull that covers it like a hard, bony helmet. Inside the brain, a special kind of cell lines the blood vessels that bring nourishment and oxygen. The cells, which form the blood-brain barrier, allow nutrient- and oxygen-rich blood to pass through to the brain. At the same time, they keep out harmful substances such as bacteria, viruses, or poisons that might disease or damage the brain. The blood-brain barrier is an extremely important protection because brain cells do not replace themselves as do other cells in the body. The brain cells we are born with must last a lifetime.

As good as the blood-brain barrier is at protecting the brain from harmful substances, it cannot keep out psychoactive chemicals such as methaqualone. Molecules from quaaludes easily pass through the blood-brain barrier, carrying their own

23

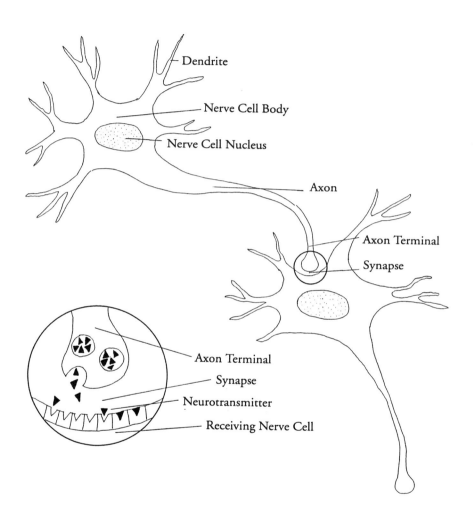

Dendrite

Nerve Cell Body

Nerve Cell Nucleus

Axon

Axon Terminal

Synapse

Axon Terminal

Synapse

Neurotransmitter

Receiving Nerve Cell

Two nerve cells or neurons are shown here. The enlarged, much simplified diagram shows neurotransmitters as they leave one nerve ending, cross the synapse, and fit into receptor slots on the receiving nerve cell.

messages, which artificially increase, prolong, or distort the neurotransmitter messages.

The brain is a very hardworking organ. Though it weighs only about 2 percent of the body's total weight, it receives about 20 percent of the body's oxygen supply.[7] At any one nanosecond (one billionth of a second), oxygen from the air we breathe and countless atoms and molecules from the foods we eat and drink are being assembled into immense numbers of biochemicals. At the same time, molecules that have already served their purpose are being broken down and recycled. Each biochemical and each action has a specific purpose in the body's smooth and healthy operation.

A wonderful balance exists in the way neurotransmitters work to convey their messages and then stop working. The brain is the organ that maintains this balance. Its billions of neurons receive messages in split-second signals from other parts of the nervous system and, in split-second timing, they respond. If you have an itch, your brain says scratch. This balance is destroyed when a psychoactive drug like quaaludes crosses the blood-brain barrier.

Quaaludes' Psychoactive Effects on the Brain

Quaaludes seem to act like a stimulant at first. They make the user feel more lively, friendlier, more confident in social settings. It is easier to approach others and to be approached by them. This is because the user is relaxed. The user's inhibitions are lowered. Quaaludes act much like alcohol.

But quaaludes' real effects are as a depressant, a downer. Relaxing, sedating effects are caused by depressing the brain's breathing and heart-regulating centers. Muscles that control speech, body movement, and hand and foot motion become relaxed. The inhibitions-lowering effect gives a long-lasting sense of euphoria, or well-being.

Depending on the amount taken, and on factors such as the user's physical and mental makeup, quaaludes can calm and relax the user, put the user to sleep, or anesthetize the user.

At larger doses, quaaludes reduce the ability to accurately sense position in space. The user has a false perception of depth and distance. Misjudging the spacing of steps, he or she may fall down a flight of stairs. Lacking a true sense of where hands and feet actually are, the user may be injured when fingers slip into mixing-bowl beaters or toes pass under lawn-mower blades. Jumping over, across, up, or down can be tricky for the user, whose sense of position is distorted. The appearance of space and distance from the top of a jump may be entirely false, as the jumper learns when the bottom is reached.

Rolling Stone magazine describes some teens, high on quaaludes after a night of hopping from one juice club to another, trying to cross the middle of an empty city street very early in the morning:

> *A group of three kids . . . stagger giggling and nodding, slip-ping and sliding . . . holding on to each other to keep from falling down—trying to get it together to cross the empty street to a cab. It takes them almost three sloppy minutes.*[8]

Fortunately for them the traffic was light at that hour. In the same report, *Rolling Stone* also explains that "wall banger" is a term that the quaalude user will probably understand very well. A wall banger is someone who repeatedly walks into walls and other objects because he or she is under the influence of a drug.

Another quaalude effect is to raise the level of pain that the brain perceives. This means that although a quaalude user may be seriously injured, he or she may feel little or no pain. The fall down a flight of stairs does not hurt at the moment. Bruises may not be felt until the next day. It has been reported that people who fall down stairs and are seriously hurt may not even notice their injury.

A burn injury may be more severe than usual because the normal feeling of pain and the sudden, natural reaction to pull away quickly from the hot object are reduced or absent. Also, the burn may go untreated because the quaalude user cannot feel pain, the body's natural warning signal.

Bones broken from a fall may not be painful to the quaalude user and may go untended. Pain from sports injuries, household accidents, and other mishaps may go unnoticed.

Quaaludes also affect the brain's ability to coordinate voluntary muscle movement. Twitching and jerking become evident as muscles contract and relax uncontrollably. This uncontrolled muscle activity is called ataxia and quaalude users who experienced it said they were "taxiing."[9] Sensations of tingling and prickling, called paresthesia, can occur in the fingertips, lips, and tongue. A user's eyes may show a symptom of quaalude abuse—an unusual "bouncing" action known to doctors (and police officers) as lateral nystagmus.

In cases of severe methaqualone poisoning, brain function is deeply depressed. There is the possibility of apnea, in which breathing stops entirely for an abnormally long period of time before resuming. Seizures, coma, and death can also occur.

Quaaludes' Effects on the Body

The quaalude user may experience a number of physical side effects. Gastrointestinal disturbances can include loss of appetite, nausea, vomiting, stomach cramps, diarrhea, or constipation. Other unwanted side effects are continued sleepiness after awakening, headache, anxiety, restlessness, and dizziness.

Quaalude use can cause changes in the small blood vessels called capillaries. This may lead to hemorrhaging in the tissue surrounding the eye and in the retina inside the eye. Stomach and intestinal hemorrhaging can also occur. The skin may develop rashes, sores, blisters, and areas of purple spotting as capillaries hemorrhage and leak blood into the skin. Skin may itch and show redness. Intense sweating can also occur.

Although quaaludes were said to be a sex-enhancing "love drug," they actually negatively affect the blood flow and muscle tension that is physically necessary for sexual performance. So while they may increase the desire for sex by lowering inhibitions, quaaludes actually decrease the user's ability to perform sexually.

When quaaludes contain impurities that are left in during sloppy bootleg manufacturing processes, the user can suffer additional and seriously damaging side effects. One common impurity, ortho-toluidine, can cause a bladder condition called necrotizing cystitis. It occurs when the healthy tissue is destroyed, leaving the bladder full of holes. Symptoms of necrotizing cystitis are nausea, vomiting, and blood in the urine.[10]

Another impurity that has been found in bootleg quaaludes is methylenedianaline, a chemical that forms during quaalude production.[11] This chemical damages the liver, which is the body's primary drug-metabolizing organ.

Quaaludes Cause Physical and Psychological Dependence

The body, under the brain's direction, works continuously to maintain itself in a state of biochemical balance. When conditions change and upset this balance, as happens when quaaludes are taken, the body adapts to the change by altering its own chemistry. The body is attempting to keep tissues, organs, and systems operating as they should for the body's well-being.

When quaaludes are abused, the body is forced to make up for the drug's continual presence and influence. In response to the drug, the body interrupts normal neurotransmitter production. Tissues are changed and organs perform differently. The respiratory and circulatory systems, which carry out breathing and blood flow, are affected.

When a user stops taking quaaludes, the body experiences symptoms of illness caused by withdrawal. These symptoms are a sign that the user's body has developed a physical dependence on quaaludes. Once the body has become physically dependent, going without quaaludes throws it into a condition known as withdrawal sickness. We will learn more about withdrawal later in this chapter.

Quaalude users can also develop psychological dependence on the drug. This means that there is a strong desire—a craving—for quaaludes in order to maintain a sense of well-being.

The user wants to take the drug again and again to get pleasure from its use or to avoid the sickness that comes from not using it.

With psychological dependence, the user may feel uneasy and anxious if he or she is unable to obtain quaaludes. When the user no longer gets the full effect from quaaludes, yet does not increase the dose, and still cannot stop using the drug, psychological dependence has occurred. People know they have become psychologically dependent on quaaludes when they begin to use quaaludes regularly and discover that they cannot stop.

Quaalude Tolerance, Loss of Tolerance, and Cross-Tolerance

Frequent use of quaaludes causes the user to develop a condition known as tolerance to the drug. This means that the user needs to take larger and larger amounts of quaaludes to get the desired effect. It can also mean that the user gets less and less of an effect each time the same amount of quaaludes is taken.

Tolerance to quaaludes develops quickly. The body develops a resistance, or tolerance, to quaaludes' sleep-inducing effects after only two weeks. Users found that the number of tablets that at first quickly put them to sleep soon needed to be increased, then increased again and again with continued use.[12] When taken for its calming, relaxing, disinhibiting effect, quaaludes were reported to be less effective after only four days.[13]

The body's ability to physically tolerate quaaludes develops more slowly than tolerance to the amount needed to produce the psychoactive effect. So as the user takes the increasingly larger amounts of quaaludes necessary for the desired mental effect, he or she gets closer and closer to the amount of quaaludes that are

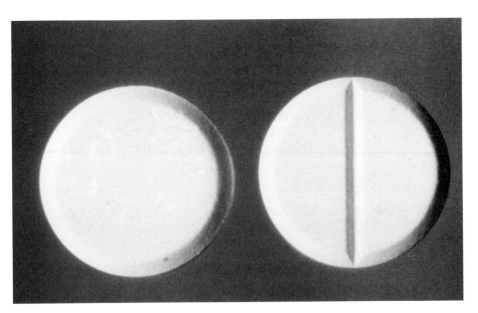

Quaalude tablets, containing the psychoactive drug methaqualone, were once made by many different pharmaceutical companies. They were taken off the market in the 1980s. Today, only counterfeit quaaludes are available.

considered a physically lethal dose—the amount that can kill. When the quaalude dose that gives the desired mental effect reaches the physically lethal dosage, breathing is depressed to the point of coma and death.

Loss of tolerance happens when a user who has reached a tolerance to high doses of quaaludes (or of any other drug), stops taking the drug, then upon returning to it at the previous high dosage, even at a much later time, experiences overdose symptoms. Overdose will be discussed later in this chapter.

Cross-tolerance is another condition that can develop with quaalude use. Cross-tolerance means that the user who has developed tolerance to quaaludes may be tolerant to other sedative-hypnotic drugs as well. This cross-tolerance occurs because the body chemistry that metabolizes quaaludes is much the same body chemistry that metabolizes other depressant, downer drugs. Cross tolerance works the other way too: tolerance to other depressants makes the user tolerant to quaaludes, also.

How the Body Metabolizes Quaaludes

Everything that enters the body is considered a foreign substance by the body's tissues and organs. So, under the brain's control, the body must determine whether the foreign substance is beneficial or will do harm.

Beneficial and useful substances, like food, water, and oxygen, are converted into biochemicals, which the body's cells use to produce energy and heat, and to build bone, muscle, blood, and organs. The body then rids itself of the waste that accumulates during this process of converting and building and energizing. If a harmful substance such as bacteria, a virus, or poison enters the body, it is neutralized—made harmless—by conversion to different, nondamaging by-products. These are then eliminated in the body's waste. The liver is the body's major drug-neutralizing organ.

The body's process of converting, using, neutralizing, and eliminating beneficial and toxic substances is called metabolism. The by-products of metabolism are called metabolites.

When quaaludes are taken they are absorbed by the stomach and intestines, then carried in the blood throughout the body and brain. Quaaludes have the greatest effect on the brain. It is in the liver, however, that quaaludes are broken down into metabolites. The metabolites are then filtered out of the blood by the kidneys, which pass them to the bladder. From the bladder, the quaalude metabolites leave the body in the urine.

The liver is a large organ, weighing about three pounds. It is composed of tightly packed cells that make a group of drug-neutralizing biochemicals called enzymes. The liver's enzymes convert poisonous drugs into harmless by-products.

The length of time the liver takes to neutralize quaaludes depends on a number of factors. The general health of the user—and especially the health of the user's liver—can influence how long quaaludes remain active. The user's age is another important factor. As people get older, they often have reduced liver efficiency. After about age thirty, a gradual decline in the liver's ability to neutralize poisonous substances begins.[14]

Women usually experience longer and stronger effects from quaaludes. Quaaludes are stored in the fatty tissues of the body. Women generally have a higher percentage of body fat than men. So we generalize that women's liver enzymes neutralize quaaludes more slowly. Heredity, too, can influence how drugs are broken down.

Quaaludes and Other Depressant Drugs

Some drugs, when taken together, boost each other's psychoactive effects. Together, they produce an effect that is greater than the sum of their individual effects. This is called synergism, or an interactive effect. Quaaludes and other depressant drugs, such as alcohol and barbiturates, have this effect when they are taken together. Drug synergism can be extremely dangerous and often fatal.

As we have learned, quaaludes are downers that work by depressing the central nervous system. Breathing slows. When another downer is taken with quaaludes, it too slows the user's breathing. But because of the drugs' synergism, the drugs act together to slow breathing more than if their single actions were simply added together. Depending on how much of the drugs are taken, the brain's breathing center can become so depressed by the drugs' boosted effects that breathing stops. Without medical attention, seizures, coma, and death can follow.

Quaaludes and alcohol have been used frequently for their combined effect. The practice is called "luding out." The respiratory failure that results from the combination of quaaludes and alcohol has been a major cause of quaalude-related deaths.[15]

34

Toxicity and Overdose With Quaaludes

People who regularly take high doses of quaaludes show signs of sluggish thought processes, general stupor, vision impairment, lack of coordination, emotional instability, and sleeplessness. With overdose, especially when other sedative-hypnotic drugs have also been taken with quaaludes, the user may experience nausea and vomiting with heavy saliva production. Respiration, heart rate, and blood pressure decrease. Muscle tone also decreases and the user has reduced responses to pain and to loud noises. The user may go into periods of apnea. He or she may slip into a coma which may last for four or five days in which the muscles are in extreme rigidness. During coma, other complications may arise. Lungs may fill with fluid and kidneys may fail. There may be bleeding in the stomach and intestines, and hemorrhaging in the retina of the eyes.[16]

Withdrawal Sickness:
When Quaaludes Use Is Stopped

A person who is physically dependent on quaaludes will undergo a variety of effects when he or she stops using the drug. Sensations not experienced while under the influence of the drug will be experienced with exaggerated intensity during withdrawal. Some users may experience irritability and headache upon suddenly stopping. No longer feeling the drug's calming, sedating effects, the withdrawing user becomes restless, twitchy, and unable to sleep. He or she may experience nausea and stomach cramps. The symptoms begin one to three days after stopping use of the drug. They may last for several days.

Other quaalude users who stop suddenly are likely to experience a full range of severe symptoms. The user's body responds with abdominal cramps, nausea, vomiting, shaking and quivering, insomnia, sweating, fever, uncontrollable blinking, cardiovascular collapse, agitation, delirium, hallucinations, disorientation, convulsions, seizures, and shock. For these quaalude users, withdrawal symptoms can occur immediately and may last for a week or more.[17]

Withdrawal is a dangerous time for the user who has become tolerant to large amounts of quaaludes. During withdrawal, sudden changes in breathing, blood pressure, and other vital processes occur. Choking and vomiting pose serious problems since throat reflexes are slowed and respiration is depressed. Vomited material may enter the lungs, causing the lungs to produce fluids which makes breathing difficult and complicates recovery.

Severe epileptic-like seizures and shock can be life-threatening during withdrawal from quaaludes. As with any sedative-hypnotic drug, withdrawal from quaaludes should never be attempted without medical supervision. Once the body's tissues have grown accustomed to quaaludes, the drug must be withdrawn slowly, during a gradual detoxification process.

The process of gradual detoxification takes place in a series of steps over a period of time. The daily dose of quaaludes is decreased every one to three days. The withdrawing user is carefully observed and monitored by doctors and nurses. Sometimes another drug is substituted for quaaludes during detoxification. Its use is gradually decreased and eventually it is withdrawn entirely.[18] Withdrawal should take place in a hospital setting with life support systems available.

Quaaludes are a powerful sedative and hypnotic drug that depress the central nervous system. They have an inhibition-lowering effect that can be quite deceptive. Their continued use can lead to tolerance, dependence, and addiction. Discontinuing quaalude use without appropriate medical supervision can be life-threatening.

Questions for Discussion

1. Why do you think it is important for the liver to remain healthy throughout a person's lifetime?

2. Discuss how quaaludes lower your inhibitions. What are some of the risks?

3. Based on your understanding of bootleg quaalude manufacture, what reasons could you give for refusing this drug if it were offered to you?

3

Quaaludes and Society

In the 1950s, a group of depressant drugs known as tranquilizers was developed. With names like Miltown™, and later Valium™ and Librium™, they came onto the market and began to be prescribed by the millions as anti-anxiety drugs. Pharmaceutical companies promoted them. Medical journals carried advertisements for them. Doctors prescribed them for those who seemed to have difficulty coping with their lives. Women, especially, were prescribed tranquilizers to help them with boredom, loneliness, or family conflicts. The message given was that if there was an anxiety or stress in one's life, there was a pill to take it away.

A Harvard University Professor, Dr. Timothy Leary, was working at the Center for Research in Personality. He began experimenting with psychoactive mushrooms, then with the hallucinogen LSD. He was dismissed from the university in 1963 when his activity became known to the faculty. Convinced that mind-altering drugs were the religion of the twenty-first century, a spiritual and artistic cure-all, he continued to promote the use of psychoactive substances. With slogans such as "The only hope is dope" and "Tune in, turn on, drop out," he appealed to the feel-good segment of society.[1]

Society and the Quaaludes Culture

Quaaludes came upon the American scene at a time of social upheaval. There was opposition and open resistance to the war in Vietnam and suspicion about our government's policies and the truthfulness of its leaders. On college campuses, figures of authority were held in contempt and rebellion against established institutions erupted. Influential public figures and celebrities encouraged rebellion against established social patterns and openly promoted the use of so-called "recreational" mind-altering drugs. The weakening of family units and breakdown of relationships within families left a growing number of young people, eager to establish independence and to try new experiences, open to turbulent forces of the times.

Quaaludes began to be made and legally prescribed in the United States in 1965. By the late 1960s, college students were using them in huge numbers. It was reported that twenty thousand quaaludes were used in three weeks at Vassar and five thousand a day were used at a Brooklyn college.[2] A period of time in the 1970s and 1980s when quaaludes were widely used has been referred to as the "Quaalude Culture."

The Quaalude Culture of the 70s and 80s is reported to have had its beginning at Ohio State University.[3] There, football players, winding down from a Saturday game, took quaaludes. Other students learned of the drug's inhibition-reducing and euphoria-producing effects. Quaalude use spread quickly. Jane*, who was a student at Ohio State in the early 70s, talks about quaaludes:

> *We called them sopers, and Ohio State was the soper capital of the world. It was a more trusting time then. There wasn't the money in drugs like there is today. You'd be at a party and someone—you didn't even know the person—would hand you a couple of pills and you'd just pop them. I liked sopers because they made you feel drunk without a hangover. And they were good for coming down from hallucinogens. I used mushrooms, and acid (LSD), and there were times when it was like "Okay, I been awake for 24 hours and my feet are still twitching." So I'd take sopers to come down. But I didn't have a death wish. I knew the danger of using alcohol with 'ludes. I never used the two together.[4]*

Quaalude use became widespread among students at the country's universities. Huge amounts of the drug were diverted to campus dealers. Jars of the pills were available at fraternities.[5] Where young people gathered, socially or politically, quaaludes were often found.[6] In New York City, at least fifteen nightclubs catered to "full-time, flat-out luders." The clubs were known as "juice bars" because in most of them the only drink available was fruit juice, especially convenient when many customers were underage. With names like "The Jungle," "The Zoo," "The

* Not her real name

41

This is one of the secret or clandestine "labs" where counterfeit quaaludes were made. This one was raided by the Drug Enforcement Agency. Quaaludes from such labs are of unknown strength and may contain toxic impurities that cause a serious bladder disease known as necrotizing cystitis.

Fudge Factory," and "Forbidden Fruit," they charged a few dollars entry fee, which entitled young patrons to a cup of juice. Sometimes favors like whistles or balloons, which would appeal to kids, were given away.[7]

High school students also had easy access to quaaludes. A seventeen year old describes his purchase: "Every day a blue van would drive up to our high school. We would run out to buy quaaludes. Then I'd take a couple and just pass out in class."[8]

A grown man today, John* tells how, as a sixteen-year-old, he acquired quaaludes, which he knew as sopers.

> *I bought them from kids already out of high school who hung around the university. The pills were bought by the hundreds, then resold. I bought and resold them, too. I took sopers in a social setting with friends. There might be a very large group of kids in one room, and everybody was taking sopers. I took them during the school day, too, to get through the day. My use was sporadic. Then I began to not like what the sopers did. I didn't get the same effect. . . ."*[9]

In the entertainment world, popular actors and musicians linked their art to the use of a variety of psychoactive substances, including quaaludes. Descriptions of addiction, overdose, and death chronicled the drug habits, abuse, and self-destruction of well-known personalities. Often their closest associates—their physicians, agents, managers, and friends—looked the other way.

Elvis Presley died on August 16, 1977 at the age of forty-two. His death was attributed to cardiac arrhythmia—irregular heartbeat—but toxicology reports revealed that many prescription

---

* Not his real name

drugs were found in his body. One of the drugs was quaaludes, found in an amount above the toxic level.

Adored by his fans, Presley relied on an elaborate schedule of drugs to get him through appearances, filming, recording, and to help him lose weight. He needed uppers to energize him for his shows. He could not fall asleep, or stay asleep, without sedative-hypnotic drugs. Then, to wake up from his drugged sleep, he needed the jolt of amphetamines. His personal physician prescribed the pills, tablets, and injections by the thousands.

In 1981, Presley's doctor, George Nichopoulos, went before the Tennessee medical examiner board because he was suspected of over-prescribing drugs to Presley. It was learned that during the last two and a half years of his life, Elvis Presley received more than nineteen thousand doses of narcotics, stimulants, sedatives, and antidepressants from Nichopoulos.[10]

Nichopoulos' license to practice medicine was suspended for three months and he was put on probation for three years, but members of the board of medical examiners nevertheless praised him for the circumstances under which he attended to Elvis Presley.[11] In 1995, many years after Presley's death, Nichopoulos lost his medical license when the state of Tennessee decided he overprescribed addictive drugs to Presley, singer Jerry Lee Lewis, and others. He was found guilty of malpractice and unethical conduct with thirteen patients.[12]

Freddie Prinze was a popular star of the 1970s whose life ended in a haze of drugs. Prinze starred in the successful television series "Chico and the Man." He was addicted to quaaludes, provided to him by a Las Vegas doctor. In 1977, at the age of twenty-three, Prinze shot himself. The day he died, he had taken half a dozen quaaludes.[13]

John Belushi was a brilliant, wild comedian. He was part of the early Saturday Night Live crew and made "The Blues Brothers" and "National Lampoon's Animal House" movies, among others. Belushi's multiple talents and hyperactive energy led him into an unrelenting and exhausting schedule of television work, film, personal appearances, and music and comedy writing. To keep on working for unnaturally long periods without sleep, and to spark and keep up a creative flow, and finally to bring himself down from prolonged drug highs, he used stimulants, sedative-hypnotics, narcotics, and alcohol in bewildering and, ultimately, deadly numbers. His creative and business associates and his friends were aware of his destructive behavior—some shared the same lifestyle—but they ignored it or condoned it. Drugs were always available on sets during filming. Although Belushi's living, travel, and household expenses were paid out by his accounting staff and he had little need for large amounts of cash, he received $2,500 a week from his studio for expenses—which, it was widely known, he used to buy the cocaine, heroin, amphetamines, marijuana, quaaludes, and other drugs he used.[14]

One of the reasons Belushi took quaaludes was to reduce the restlessness that came with a cocaine high. But there were times when he was so drugged that his unsteady legs and slurred speech nearly caused performances to be canceled.[15] In 1982, at the age of thirty-three, Belushi died of a drug overdose.

Society's Attitude Towards Quaaludes

Society's attitude toward a drug influences its availability. In turn, the drug's effects on society may influence its use or non-use. So it was with quaaludes.

Quaaludes came on the market advertised as a safe and non-addicting sleeping aid. Immediately, they became a very popular drug. A large market of anxious, stressed-out, and poorly sleeping people created a demand for the drug which was not supposed to have the negative side effects of other prescribed sleeping pills available at the time.

Pharmaceutical companies, promoting quaaludes' advantages, made large profits on the drug. Sales increased 360 percent in 1972. A 150 milligram tablet was produced at a cost of about four cents.[16] Annual sales in the United States were reported at ten million dollars by 1972.[17]

As quickly as quaalude use spread among consumers who needed the drug for medical reasons, a large market of so-called recreational quaalude users also developed. Even though quaaludes could be obtained legally only by prescription, the recreational user found the drug widely available and easy to get.

Some quaaludes were bought from people who had contact with drug warehouse workers who stole the drug, especially imperfect pills or capsules that were being returned for reprocessing.[18] Some quaaludes were obtained when word spread, identifying certain "scrip" or "script" doctors who would prescribe the pills in large numbers over and over again to the same individuals, and pharmacists who would fill the prescriptions again and again with no questions asked. There was a great deal of money to be made. One "scrip doc" was investigated for prescribing 45,000 tablets in one month.[19] These doctors were not respected by the people who used them to get their drugs, but they made a lot of money. One young man describes his eventual quaalude addiction:

Pins and buttons can carry a quick message. This button was given to a young university woman in the 1970s who decided not to follow its suggestion.

I started taking Quaalude[s] after seeing a doctor. He just kept prescribing Quaalude[s] for me, more and more Quaalude[s]. He's a real scrip doctor, you know; everybody . . . knows his name. But I didn't go to him for a high. I just wanted something to help me sleep, 'cause I never was much of a good sleeper.[20]

A pharmacist told about his quaalude sales:

I could retire on what I make on it. A lot of drugstores will deny they carry Quaaludes on the phone. You tell people you have it and an hour later they just float in here, their feet hardly touching the ground. Most of the people who come in have phony [or forged] prescriptions. Sometimes, I'm forced to say I've already sold out.[21]

There were legitimate doctors, of course, who prescribed quaaludes in good faith, believing their patients were getting a safe and effective medicine. The *Physicians' Desk Reference*, from which doctors take much of their information about the drugs they prescribe, at first said nothing about quaaludes' potential for addiction. "The poor overworked doc gets big boxes of samples from the drug company, looks up in the *PDR* [*Physician's Desk Reference*] and nothing there says it's addictive, it looks clean, and so he starts passing them out. He doesn't know he's doing anything harmful," relates a doctor in a drug treatment center in the 1970s, prior to quaaludes' classification as a controlled substance.[22]

In one clinic survey, it was found that almost all the quaalude-abusing-patients interviewed were first introduced to the drug by legal prescription or by a person who had access to "legal" prescriptions.[23]

48

With demand growing for the increasingly popular quaaludes (heightened by media reports which unintentionally glamorized the new "love drug"), and as reclassification to a controlled substance made the drug harder to get, a thriving black market quickly developed. The drug underworld stepped in, filling the demand with illegally made, smuggled, and counterfeit quaaludes. In 1981, about a billion illegally obtained tablets were consumed. Selling on the black market at an average of six dollars each, it was a $6-billion-a-year business.[24] In Miami, Florida, quaaludes were being dealt so openly that sales were rung up directly on the cash registers used in the bars, clubs, and lounges where quaaludes were being sold.[25]

Warnings About Quaaludes

Warnings about quaaludes' addictive properties came from countries that began marketing the drug years before the United States. Cases of abuse were reported in Japan as early as the 1950s.[26] In the mid-1960s, it was reported that half the drug addicts in Japanese hospitals were on quaaludes and widespread quaalude abuse was reported in Japan in 1969.[27] In 1962, the first reported overdose death occurred in Germany.[28] A number of suicides related to quaaludes were also reported in Germany, where methaqualone was available without prescription.[29] Great Britain observed cases of physical and psychological dependence on quaaludes in 1966.[30] Australia also reported quaalude problems.

In the United States in 1972, 275 cases of acute methaqualone intoxication were reported, with 16 of them resulting in death.[31] *U.S. News & World Report* stated in 1973, "Methaqualone is blamed for at least 313 overdoses and 53 suicides in a 16-month period."[32] In 1974, eighty-eight people died from quaalude overdoses in the United States.[33] Emergency-room visits associated with quaaludes between May 1976 and April 1977 were estimated at fifty-five hundred.[34] When Broward County, Florida, began routine urine testing of intoxicated drivers in 1980, they found that 82 percent of them had been taking quaaludes.[35]

Writing in 1973 in reply to the Pharmaceutical Manufacturers Association, Peter J. Ognibene says "The methaqualone boom has only just begun: distribution increased 1500 percent in five years; one company's distribution of 300 milligram tablets jumped from eight million in 1968 to over 100 million last year (1971). Aggressive advertising and the drug's illicit popularity would seem better explanations for this increase than the relatively stable need for insomnia prescriptions."[36]

Quaaludes remained an uncontrolled drug, then a Schedule II drug, long after its dangers were recognized and warnings were given. It took from the late 1960s until 1982 for legislators to reclassify quaaludes from an uncontrolled drug to a Schedule II drug, then two more years—to 1984—to finally classify it as an illegal Schedule I substance. Influencing the reluctance to reclassify was the pharmaceutical industry's stand that quaaludes were not a serious substance of abuse, but rather a safe and useful drug when used properly. An attitude of acceptance, by many people, of drugs as simply a part of growing up, was also influential. The attitude toward quaaludes had to change sufficiently to help bring about laws that would make the manufacture and prescription of quaaludes illegal, and that would impose penalties when the law was broken.

Quaaludes' Toll on Society

Quaalude abuse took its toll on society in many ways. Peoples' health and safety were affected. Emergency rooms admitted not only abusers suffering from quaalude overdose and withdrawal, injuries in automobile accidents, drownings, and suicide attempts related to the impaired judgment caused by quaalude; they also treated people who were innocently involved in accidents caused by the impaired judgment of the quaalude user and women involved in quaalude-related date rapes.

Criminal activity in the drug-related black market and the corruption it fostered also took a toll on society. The huge amounts of money to be made from illegal quaaludes lured public officials, doctors, pharmacists, sports figures, and everyday citizens into corruption. A champion speedboat racer, George Morales, was sentenced to sixteen years in prison for smuggling methaqualone and other drugs into the country between 1980 and 1986, and for tax evasion.[37] Baseball player Joe Pepitone was convicted and sentenced for possession of hundreds of quaaludes.[38] A group of elderly men was arrested and charged with dealing in hundreds of thousands of quaaludes.[39]

Drug money paid for yachts and condominiums. Expensive purchases were made with huge cash payments and no questions asked. Immense amounts of illegal drug money were taken secretly out of the country. After being deposited in foreign banks, the "laundered" money, its drug origins concealed, then returned to the United States for investment in legitimate businesses and real estate.[40]

Society also suffered the loss of talents of people whose motivation and goals were dulled, whose potential for achievement

51

Patent medicines for every kind of sickness imaginable were used in the nineteenth century. These containers from around the world indicate some of the things people were taking.

was diminished, by the sedative-hypnotic effects of their quaalude use.

Jane, the Ohio State student who earlier described her use of quaaludes and other drugs, reflects on that time of her life: "What should I have been doing while I was in college? I should have been working to get into medical school. But I blew it with the drugs. So today I'm not a doctor. . . . [T]here was a potential there that I missed."[41]

Another case tells of a twenty-year-old man who used "sopors" for his anxiety. His tolerance to quaaludes increased to the point where he would use five tablets and alcohol and still feel somewhat anxious. He described getting the "shakes" even after taking sopers. He also noted increased forgetfulness, anxiety, episodes of headache, anorexia, and an "upset equilibrium" when he didn't take methaqualone. With daily soper use, he began to have excessive stress in his social environment. He lost his job, his girlfriend, and much of what he called his "ego strength" after two weeks of daily methaqualone abuse.[42]

Quaaludes in Today's Society

Today, quaaludes are classified as a Schedule I substance under the Federal law known as the Controlled Substances Act, Title II of the Comprehensive Drug Abuse Prevention and Control Act of 1970. Classification as a Schedule I substance categorizes quaaludes as:

> • *A drug that has a high potential for abuse.*
>
> • *A drug that has no currently accepted medical use in treatment in the United States.*
>
> • *A drug that lacks accepted safety for use under medical supervision.*

Under the Controlled Substances Act, it is illegal to traffic in quaaludes or any other drug containing methaqualone. This means it is against the law to manufacture, distribute, possess, dispense, or prescribe the drug. The law applies to all of the numerous and variously named methaqualone-containing "Quaaludes," "sopors," "ludes," or "quacks." It places them in the same category—Schedule I—as heroin.

People found guilty of trafficking in quaaludes can be sentenced to prison and be charged with fines. Federal trafficking penalties vary. The length of time in prison and the size of the fine depend on the amount of drug involved, whether death or serious injury resulted in the quaalude trafficking, and whether it was a first or second offense.[43]

The Drug Enforcement Agency's Drug Demand Reduction Division reports about twenty quaalude cases a year, far below the number of cases reported during the Quaalude Culture years. It has been pointed out, however, that drug preferences appear to occur in ten-year cycles, alternating between downer/depressants and upper/stimulant drugs. Heroin and sedative-downers are making a comeback in the 90s.

The growing popularity of Rohypnol, the newly-arrived sedative made in Europe, illustrates the trend toward downer abuse in the 90s. Rohypnol, also known as roofies, rope, and roach is in a class of sedatives that includes Valium. Its effects are stronger and more powerful than Valium or quaaludes.[44] Its sedative effects can last for eight hours or longer. Police in Florida, where roofies were first reported, describe how, when roofie-abusing drivers are stopped for their extremely poor driving, they open the car door and just fall out.[45]

Roofies have a deceiving appearance, police and drug counselors say. They are packaged like other medicines and look harmless. Teens find them affordable and the drugs are available from classmates and friends.[46]

Rohypnol can cause amnesia, or the loss to short-term memory. A case is described in which a girl's date gave her the drug with some alcohol. When the drug wore off hours later, the girl had no memory of having had sex. It was not until she discovered that she was pregnant that she realized what had happened.[47]

As Rohypnol's popularity spreads, there is concern that cocaine and marijuana traffickers will distribute it and that dealers will try to hook children on it.[48]

One change in drug abuse in our society over the past thirty years is that the age of a person's first use has been gradually dropping. While high school seniors are reducing illegal drug use, eighth graders are slowly increasing drug use.[49]

Knowing about quaaludes' effects on the individual and on society as a whole, helps people develop an informed opinion about why they should not become involved with drugs. It also provides the basis for questioning future persuasive voices which may promote quaaludes or a drug like it.

Questions for Discussion

1. What reasons can you give for quaaludes' popularity among students?

2. What signs of a "feel-good" society do you see today?

3. Identify factors which may cause society to change its attitude toward a popular substance, product, or activity.

4

Getting Personal: How Quaaludes Can Affect You

Earlier in this book you learned that your brain is "command central" for your body's every move. The rate and depth of every breath you take and the rate and strength of your every heartbeat are established by an immense number of intricately related messages between body and brain.

The pressure at which blood flows through the arteries, veins, and capillaries that extend from your scalp to your toes is regulated in your brain. The digestive juices that enter your stomach, and the time they take to convert the food you have eaten into the next stage of nourishment, are under your brain's control. The neurotransmitter proteins that signal you to relax and sleep are programmed into being by your brain, as are the proteins that become the hormones that regulate your growth and development. What you will be as a person lies within your brain's ten billion firing neurons. The way your brain commands makes you different from everyone else.

Different People Can React Differently to Quaaludes

A person's physical makeup can greatly influence the effects of a drug like quaaludes. A small, lightweight person will most likely react differently to the same amount of quaaludes than a larger, heavier person will. Body weight makes a difference.

Your personal biochemistry also makes a difference. Some people produce more and some people produce fewer, of the natural neurotransmitters that carry messages from one nerve ending to another. The effects of a psychoactive drug such as quaaludes, which increases, decreases, or sustains the effects of natural neurotransmitters, vary from one person to another.

Gender makes a difference, too. The hormones that make boys into men and girls into women cause other body differences, also. Girls and women are usually smaller in stature and weigh less than boys and men, and they naturally tend to have a higher percentage of body fat than boys and men. The drug in quaaludes is stored for a longer time in fatty tissues of the body.

Age can also play a role. A young person, probably because he or she is still developing in size, emotional maturity, and sexuality, may respond to quaaludes in a way quite different from a fully developed adult's response. If you are still growing, your cells are rapidly dividing. Bone length and muscle mass, blood volume and your overall size are undergoing change. Emotional development is in progress also. This can be complicated by a developing sexuality with hormonal changes that contribute to mood swings. Adding quaaludes' chemistry into the young person's own already rapidly changing biochemistry may produce some odd and unwanted results.

The user's psychological makeup can be another contributing factor in quaaludes' effects. Is the user a shy person who finds it difficult to be comfortable in a social setting? What sense of self-esteem does he or she have? Is there a need to substitute quaaludes' "downer" effect for personal feelings or situations that are difficult to deal with? Does he or she think taking the drug will solve personal problems? An adventurous risk taker may try quaaludes for the curiosity of it, or use it as a party drug. A depressed user may come to rely on the drug to get through bad times, thereby removing opportunities to work through the problems that are probably the source of the depression. Quaaludes and alcohol have been used as a suicide method in some cases.

The user's frame of mind, the unconscious expectation about the drug's effects (called the "set"), as well as the setting in which quaaludes are used, may also influence reaction to the drug's effects. Taking the drug as an act of rebellion can contribute to an experience quite different from taking it in a spirit of curious experimentation. The unconscious expectation of the drug's pleasant or unpleasant effects may contribute to how a drug is experienced.

"Setting" refers to the environment in which a drug is taken. It is the physical location, the social atmosphere, and cultural attitude at the time of drug use. In other words, setting is where you are, who you are with, and what the prevailing attitude is.

Taking the drug in a setting which is perceived as safe, with good friends around, may produce effects totally different than taking drugs in an unfamiliar setting with strangers.[1]

Who Has Taken Quaaludes and Why

The reasons for taking any drug can be as varied as the people taking it. Some of the reasons given for using quaaludes have to do with personal behaviors that can almost always be changed without the use of psychoactive drugs. People who have occasional bouts of sleeplessness—insomnia—can try to change their sleep habits. By including exercise or physical activity in each day (but not too vigorously just before bedtime), they can improve their health and sense of well-being. They can also consume fewer stimulant drinks and foods, such as coffee or colas or even chocolate. By establishing a routine of "winding down" with relaxing activity before bed, they can prepare themselves for the onset of natural sleep.

For people with persistent insomnia, doctors believe that other, underlying conditions, such as depression or anxiety, cause the inability to sleep. In these cases, recognizing the cause of the depression or anxiety and learning how to eliminate it is necessary. Psychiatric therapy may be required, sometimes in conjunction with the medically-supervised use of a prescribed sleep aid, until the person is back on track.[2]

When drugs are used to escape from a troubled or hectic lifestyle, or to shield one's self from painful emotions, they chemically conceal causes that should be discovered and corrected. "They [the drugs] bypass the real work that needs to be done: emotional commitment, communication, caring and

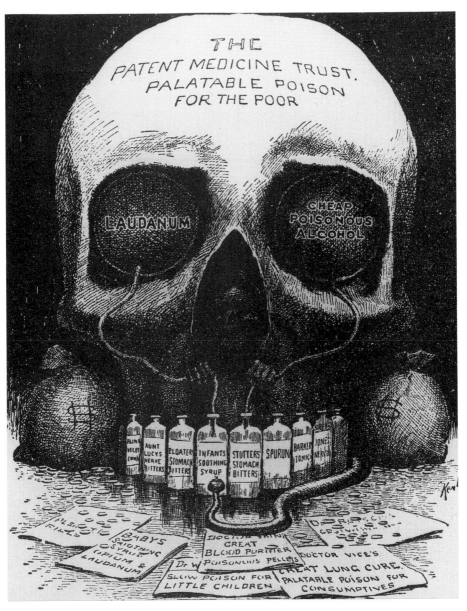

The widespread use of patent medicines meant that teething babies were being "soothed" with narcotic-containing syrups, and "tonics" laced with opium were used as cures for everything from gum disease to tuberculosis. This cartoon illustrated a series of articles about the dangers of patent medicines which appeared in *Collier's Weekly* in 1905. It was instrumental in the passage of the Pure Food and Drug Act of 1906.

affection, dealing with childhood traumas, and learning to be an adult."[3]

Using drugs is sometimes a young person's way to declare that he or she is in control of his or her own life. It appears to make a statement that "I am responsible for my own decisions." People are usually respected if they have control and are responsible for their own decisions. Having respect, especially the respect of peers, is very important. But decisions are based on choices we make. Drug abuse is *never* a good choice.

Being accepted by a peer group is one of the nicest things that can happen to a young person. It provides a comfortable base for social activities. Great value is attached to "belonging." But at the same moment that teens are in need of social group approval, they are also going through physical and emotional changes that make them feel self-conscious and easily embarrassed. They may also feel awkward in group situations for which they are still learning social skills.

Some teens may be tempted to ease their feelings of embarrassment, self-consciousness, and awkwardness with quaaludes. This lowers inhibitions and lets the user feel more at ease at parties and other group events. However, when they cover up their awkward feelings with a mind-altering drug, they deprive themselves of opportunities to learn to become socially competent. They do not discover good ways to become part of a peer group that does not use drugs. Some teens slide into a peer group that is recognized for its drug use because it is easy to get into the group and because a common interest—the use of illegal drugs— is shared.

Are Quaaludes Really a "Love Drug?"

Quaaludes gained a reputation as a "love drug" because they enhanced the desire for sex.[4] The enhanced sexual desire, however, is produced not by the complex, genuine emotions of love and caring. Instead, it is caused by a lowering of inhibitions brought on by quaalude's depressive action on the central nervous system. The user may feel a strong desire for sex and be less nervous about engaging in a sexual encounter.

However, because quaaludes depress the central nervous system, they also relax muscles and lower blood pressure and blood flow. The body becomes less able to respond sexually. Men taking quaaludes may feel a strong desire for sex and initiate the action, but the relaxed muscles and decreased blood pressure from the quaaludes interferes with the ability to perform. They do not function well sexually and in some cases may not function sexually at all. Describing his experience with quaaludes, a young man says, "All your inhibitions are definitely broken down —like everything else in your body."[5]

Another quaalude user, after two weeks of daily methaqualone abuse, described how the drug made him feel: "A stumbling euphoria and a sense of not caring. . . . They [the quaaludes] get you physically down but psychologically up. . . . I got a tingling sensation all over my body."[6]

Women who take quaaludes for its disinhibiting effects may become very desirous of sex, yet the drug's effects can reduce their ability to perform sexually as well. For both men and women, when increasingly large amounts of quaaludes are taken with greater frequency, there is no "love drug" effect. Instead the result is one of apathy and sexual problems.

Some people believe that sexual sensitivity is heightened when quaaludes and alcohol are used together. But this "luding out" actually produces a loss of sensitivity, numbness in the lips and tongue, and a general loss of coordination. The combination of double depressants—alcohol and quaaludes—is a dangerous one with serious, possibly deadly, results.

The desire for sex is psychologically complicated. It is rooted in emotions and feelings which cause our bodies to produce our own personal drugs. The desire that comes from the emotions and feelings linked to loving and caring for someone is much more important to sexual functioning than the chemically-induced desire of any so-called "love drug."

Consequences of Using Quaaludes

Look for a moment at the effects quaaludes can have when they cross the blood-brain barrier and begin to influence the user's personal chemistry:

- *They give a feeling of euphoria.*
- *They lower inhibitions.*
- *They raise the pain threshold.*
- *They impair behavior.*
- *They give a feeling of invincibility.*
- *They heighten senses.*
- *They increase sexual desire.*
- *They intensify emotions.*
- *They "expand consciousness."*

Now consider some of the consequences of each of those effects: With quaalude euphoria, there is often a feeling of invincibility. Anything seems possible. The user feels indestructible. When inhibitions are lowered, the user's judgment changes. The usual sense of awareness and self protection that keeps a person safe is diminished. With quaaludes distorting the user's perceptions through euphoria and lowered inhibition, it may seem perfectly okay to jump into high-risk activities that can lead to injury.

Quaaludes raise the user's threshold of pain. Numbness and tingling replace usual feelings. The user may not even realize the extent to which he or she has been hurt or is being hurt. An unfelt injury may go untreated at a critical time. The user also may have a reduced sense of the pain he or she is inflicting on someone else.

Quaaludes' tendency to heighten sexual desire by lowering inhibitions can lead to risky sexual encounters. The result may be an unwanted pregnancy or a sexually transmitted disease including AIDS. A willingness to participate in dangerous sexual practices may surface. Sexual assault may become more prevalent since a male quaalude user, with his inhibitions lowered and his desire raised, is likely to behave in a way that could lead to rape.[7]

When quaalude use impairs behavior, certain tasks and activities become dangerous. Driving a car, operating machinery, and participating in sports can be hazardous to the user as well as the people nearby. Automobile accidents, diving accidents, drownings, and deliberate and accidental suicides have been linked to quaalude use.

The emotions felt when under quaaludes' influence can be greatly intensified for some users. This is considered a positive drug reaction by people who think that such heightened sensibility helps them creatively or emotionally or sexually. But chemically-boosted emotions can be so artificially heightened that feelings of rage, anger, hatred, aggression, and despair are expressed in actions that are violent, antisocial, or self-destructive. The "expanded consciousness" of a quaaludes high can turn out to be no consciousness at all.

Experimenting with drugs can upset emotional growth. It may be slowed down, stopped, or even reversed.[8] Drug treatment counselors, doctors, and psychiatrists tell of patients who are well into their adult years yet lack maturity. They may have reached a certain level of maturity, then a drug habit interfered with further development or wiped out the maturity that had been achieved. They remain at a childlike level.

A long-term study of depressant drug abusers whose drugs included quaaludes, indicated that sedative abusers developed increased symptoms of depression, difficulties in vocabulary and abstract reasoning, and anxiety.[9]

Being dependent on a drug like quaaludes takes constant attention. Where is the next pill coming from? How will it be obtained? How will it be paid for? It takes a lot of time, energy, and money to meet the demands of a drug habit. The drug's demands get in the way of developing emotional maturity and growth. The personal freedom to experience, to participate, and to accomplish things in life becomes limited by the demands of the drug and its effects on the user.

Quaaludes and other drugs can also place limitations on how a person uses his or her natural intelligence and coordination. Jane, the Ohio State University student, was in her early twenties in the 1970s when quaaludes were the rage on American campuses.

Dating from the 1500s, this Aztec statue of Xochipilli, the Prince of Flowers, was found buried on the slopes of the Mexican volcano Popocatepetl. The euphoric prince and the pedestal he sits on are covered with symbols representing hallucinogenic plants, such as a mushroom cap, a morning glory vine, and a tobacco flower.

As Jane related in Chapter 3, her use of quaaludes and other drugs took away her motivation to study for the medical career she wanted. She stopped using drugs when she recognized the toll they were taking on her mental and physical coordination:

> You want to know why I decided to stop doing all the drugs? Let me tell you. I was living in this apartment and we had a mouse. So one day I spread a mouse trap with peanut butter and set the thing. I was sliding it under the refrigerator when it snapped on my thumb. That really hurt. But okay, after a few minutes I reset the trap and was sliding it under the refrigerator again. And again I did the same thing. Sprung the trap on the same thumb. Dumb, huh? But the thing is, I'm not dumb. "That's it," I thought. I'm off the drugs.[10]

The Body's Own Drugs

For a long time, scientists suspected that the body produces some type of substance that operates in the central nervous system to provide pain protection. Since the 1970s, such substances have been identified. They are described as "endogenous morphine-like substances" and are called "endorphins," a contraction of the words endogenous and morphine.[11]

Endorphins act as our own personal endogenous drugs. They are called endogenous drugs because they are made by our bodies within our bodies. Drugs like quaaludes, that come from outside the body, are considered exogenous drugs. Endogenous drugs are produced in response to the brain's perception of excitement, happiness, warmth, love, pain, fear, anger, and the other many sensations, feelings, and emotions we experience.

Some endogenous drugs can make us feel relaxed and sexually stimulated, provide a sense of euphoria, or create an expanded consciousness or "connectedness" similar to quaaludes. The big difference is that endogenous drugs come into being under our own biochemistry and their effects are more subtle than the fast, chemically intense high of drugs that come from outside the body. The personal high of endogenous drugs occurs when something stimulates the brain to increase the production of endorphins. Ways to call up, or to achieve the good feelings of our endogenous drugs can be learned. Some people increase the production of their endogenous drugs by running or meditating, or by working on something that brings their imagination or creativity into play. The thrill of victory, accomplishment, or sudden discovery, the pleasure of having a good time with good friends, or of feeling competent—all of these can stimulate the production of pleasure-giving endogenous drugs.

Understanding who we are and discovering what we want in our lives are useful tools for learning how to stimulate the good feelings generated by our own endogenous drugs. Becoming self-reliant and defining personal values are other useful tools. Acquiring these tools can be hard work. Sometimes the path to acquiring them gets obscured—or revealed—by the way we are spoken to and treated as small children, by the series of influential life events that happen to us, and by the people whose lives touch ours. In the quest for self-understanding and personal discovery, we might get confused or lost. We might wish for quick self-knowledge, easy answers, and clear and direct solutions to problems, possibly through a drug-expanded consciousness.

Some people have thought that the highs produced by quaaludes provide such an expanded consciousness. But experience has shown that relying on exogenous chemicals for self-understanding doesn't give a true and reliable sense of who and what we are and what we can become. That can come only from within ourselves.

Friendship and Quaaludes

When asked where they obtained quaaludes, people often answered "A friend gave them to me" or "from a friend who had connections." Drug sharing among friends during the Quaalude Culture of the 1970s was considered generous by many people at the time. But real friends who care about each other do not share their drug habits. Friends who see their friends getting into drug trouble speak out. They show their friendship by expressing concern, offering to listen, offering help, getting help. It takes courage, and the willingness to take a risk, and sometimes it does not work out well. Friends may be offended, or turned off by others' concerns for them. But the strong person takes the risk.

Robin Williams was John Belushi's friend. Williams talks about friendship and drugs at the time of John Belushi's death:

> It takes a real good friend to say 'Stop.' If you do, perhaps you'll lose a friend. I wasn't strong enough, man enough, to say it. I think people are afraid of the commitment of getting involved in someone else's life, even if they are ending it before your eyes." [12]

Questions for Discussion

1. Name ten activities that you and your classmates are involved in. Describe how each might be limited by the effects of quaaludes.

2. Describe the feelings of a personal "high" that you experienced because you were happy, proud, excited, victorious, creative, or successful. Discuss ways that personal highs can be achieved without the use of a psychoactive drug.

3. Discuss why you think being good at a certain activity is a source of good feelings.

5

Quaaludes and the Family

Each of us began our life as a single cell which came into existence when our mother's egg cell and our father's sperm cell became one. That first single cell contained forty-six chromosomes. Twenty three came from mom and twenty three came from dad.

Within the chromosomes are our genes and the DNA that lays down instructions for building the many body and brain proteins into the person that each of us becomes. Everyone becomes someone different. You are the receiver of a genetic heritage that is uniquely yours.

Genetic makeup determines physical characteristics, temperament, and biochemistry. Are your fingernails long and oval in shape or short and square? Do you laugh easily or are you a more serious type? What is your personal chemistry? Do you digest a big meal quickly and feel hungry soon after? Or does a little food seem to satisfy you for a long time?

Your unique genetic heritage influences how you will metabolize any food, drink, medicine, or drug that you put into your body. Genetic inheritance can also influence the tendency to abuse psychoactive drugs such as quaaludes.

Genetic Tendency to Problems With Drugs

The genetic building code that we inherit from our parents determines what levels of enzymes and hormones our bodies will produce, as well as which neurotransmitters will be supplied abundantly and which may be scarce. The levels and activity of enzymes, hormones, and neurotransmitters affect how the body and brain respond to substances that enter them.

Studies have shown that some families have a genetic vulnerability to alcoholism. If one parent is an alcoholic, the chances that a child will also become alcoholic increase. If both parents are alcoholic, the percentage increases further.[1] Susceptible family members lack or are deficient in enzymes necessary for alcohol metabolism. The unmetabolized alcohol does not leave the body, but recirculates, causing stronger or prolonged reactions.

Evidence suggests that families can have a genetic vulnerability to other drugs, also. While genes do not directly determine who may become drug dependent, the presence or absence of certain genes does influence the body's ability to produce drug-metabolizing

73

biochemicals that may influence the tendency to become drug dependent.[2]

Some ethnic groups have an inherited deficiency in certain drug-metabolizing enzymes, which makes them more susceptible to drug dependence. Native Americans can have severe side effects to alcohol. Suicide is one of the sad results. The mortality rate from alcohol abuse for fifteen- to twenty-four-year-old Native Americans in New Mexico is reported to be fifty times higher than the Caucasian rate.[3] Asians, also, can have a more pronounced side effect to alcohol than Caucasians. They tend to metabolize alcohol more slowly, which can cause nausea and flushing of the face.[4] Quaaludes, which are depressants with effects similar to alcohol, are metabolized similarly to alcohol. They may be reasonably thought to cause some of the same side effects in vulnerable ethnic groups' members.

Genetic inheritance may also influence how severely a drug's side effects are felt. In some people, a drug's negative effects may be reduced or minimized. If a person's genetic makeup lets him or her use a drug without suffering negative side effects, the person may use more of the drug or use it more frequently.[5]

Personality traits that increase the tendency to drug use may also be influenced by genetic inheritance. The impulsive person who keeps repeating behavior that got him or her into trouble previously, who values the immediate effects of a drug more than he or she respects the long-term negative consequences of its use, may have such personality traits.[6] The personality that is open to experimentation with drugs, that takes risks, may have a genetic base for its tendency to drug abuse and dependence. Issues of self-esteem, sense of control, and feelings of depression also figure into the overall picture of family genetics.

But genetic inheritance is not the only family influence on the tendency to use drugs. The family environment is also influential. Even if a person has inherited a tendency for developing drug dependence, the person will not become drug dependent if no drugs are available in the person's environment, and no drugs are ever used.[7]

The Family Environment

The family environment consists of many factors and conditions that form outside the individual and may influence his or her behavior. It includes all the people in the family as well as nonrelatives who are significant and have an influence on the family.

A family's environment is also the atmosphere created by the way family members relate to each other and how they communicate their feelings, ideas, and wishes to each other. Environment includes living conditions, the availability and use of financial and other resources, and attitudes toward the use and management of resources.

Parents' attitudes toward health, beliefs, and discipline, as well as their giving of praise, recognition, and approval, are all part of the family environment. The availability of drugs as well as parents' and other family members' attitudes about drug use and abuse also play a part in the family environment.

Within the family, the parents' attitude toward the use of legal drugs such as alcohol conveys certain messages and can influence a teen's attitude and behavior toward drugs. A teenager describes his use of quaaludes: "My parents never knew I was taking ludes. When I came home zonked out on ludes, I'd just say I was drunk on beer."[8]

Ads for quaalude-related merchandise as they appeared in issues of *High Times* magazine in the 1970s are shown here. T-shirts, lockets, and even a bar of soap shaped like a large quaalude tablet could be mail ordered.

How a family handles stress can influence children's ideas about drug use. If parents rely on the use of alcohol, tranquilizers, sleeping pills, or other sedative-type drugs, for calming down or relaxing, they give the message that it is preferable to get through difficult situations and stressful times by chemically changing their mood. (More than 150 million prescriptions for sedative-hypnotic drugs are written in the United States each year.[9]) Children learn that if pills can take away discomfort, you do not have to suffer through a tough time. But in such an environment, family members also reduce their opportunities to practice communicating, to learn coping skills or to resolve problems. Children have fewer examples of how to work through a difficult situation or problem. They miss out on the personal strength to be gained by learning to express their worries and needs, and by dealing constructively with disappointment or frustration or failure.

In a family where parents look the other way when it comes to teens' illegal drug use, teens are likely to be aware and accepting of drug abuse.[10] It has also been found that when the family environment includes a sibling who uses drugs, there is an increase in younger children's decision to try drugs.[11] Research indicates that the age of first use is a strong predictor of future drug abuse: when drug use begins before age fifteen, serious abuse problems are likely to occur later.[12]

Good parenting skills make use of the fact that children develop in stages. One stage must be mastered before another stage can be entered successfully. If parents do not understand this, they may have unrealistic expectations for their childrens' developmental levels. A child who is expected to perform or behave beyond his or her age or ability may be made to feel a sense of personal failure. Low self-esteem follows close behind. A low sense of self-esteem is recognized as a contributing factor in leading kids to experiment with drugs.[13]

Inconsistent parental discipline is another family risk factor in drug use, as are confusing or relaxed rules about the use of alcohol, tobacco, and other drugs.[14] Children who live in an unsupervised environment where they must care for themselves, where there is little parental involvement in their lives, and where they do not experience warmth and closeness are at risk for drug use. During the years of the Quaalude Culture, rapid changes were occurring in society. In larger numbers than in other historical periods, parents withdrew from their children's lives. Young people came to depend more on their peers for security and approval. The atmosphere enabled large numbers of high school students to gather freely to party with quaaludes, which were easy to find. "They're everywhere—in schools, at parties, in bars," one teen said. Another said she started taking quaaludes when she was twelve, but she saw younger and younger kids, kids in elementary school, taking them. A child was seen selling quaaludes to the cars stopped at a traffic light.[15]

Parents sometimes accept the idea that their children's experimentation with drugs is a normal part of growing up, that everybody is taking drugs. But drug experimentation is drug use, and drug use can carry significant risk. In some families, "parents ignore drug use out of love, lack of awareness, or willful blindness."[16]

The children of families that live in dangerous, threatening environments are at risk for drug use. It is believed that constant emotional and physical stresses during childhood years, which can produce fear, anxiety, anger, and loss of self esteem, can change how a person's brain functions. Being constantly afraid, for example, may cause changes in neurons, or nerve cells. These changes may then cause an increased tendency to develop new fears.[17]

Drug-using families often have a great deal of instability. They may move often, causing them to be socially isolated frequently. They usually do not get to know neighbors and others well before they move on to a new location. Children generally have little or no bonding with their schools. The family is generally cut off from institutions or people that might be helpful.

The drug-using family is also less likely to establish rituals that create bonds between parents and children, brothers and sisters. The simple rituals of being together at certain times of the day, of eating together, of sharing family work and play, are absent. Special occasions and moments of celebration or recognition are not always observed. There are few reoccurring events that everybody in the family looks forward to that enhance family cohesiveness and provide a sense of stability.

Other family stresses that contribute to drug-use risk are worries about money, employment, and career decisions. Disagreements over relationships, and conflict and violence among family members as well, can also place them at risk for drug use and abuse. The positive influences that children need to help them build resistance to drugs are all too often scarce in the lives of children in drug-using families.[18]

Quaaludes and Pregnancy

Sedative-hypnotic drugs such as quaaludes depress the breathing centers in the brain. One of the results is that the rate of respiration is reduced. This is especially dangerous during pregnancy because with less oxygen entering the mother's lungs, there is a reduced oxygen supply to the fetus. Deprived of oxygen, the fetus's brain, which is in a rapid and critical state of development, can be damaged.

If a pregnant woman goes into withdrawal from quaaludes, she may enter labor prematurely. This means the baby will be born too soon, before it is fully developed and is big enough. The leading cause of infant death in the United States is due to low birth weight.[19]

Crossing The Placental Barrier

In Chapter Two we learned that psychoactive drugs such as quaaludes cross the blood-brain barrier and cause changes in brain function. Quaaludes also cross the placental barrier. This means the drug can cause changes in the developing fetus.

During pregnancy, a disc-shaped organ called the placenta develops and attaches to the inner wall of the uterus. The fetus, or embryo, is attached to the placenta by an umbilical cord which contains the fetus's blood vessels. The placenta permits oxygen and nourishment to pass from the mother's blood to the fetus's blood, but the placenta is lined with special cells that act as a barrier to harmful substances. This barrier protects the fetus as it grows and develops during its nine months in the mother's uterus.

However, the placental barrier cannot keep out molecules of psychoactive drugs. Some drug molecules are able to penetrate the placental cell barrier. This means that drugs in the mother's blood pass into the fetus's blood. So the developing fetus's blood supply—its source of life—then contains not only oxygen and nourishment, but also whatever drugs the mother happens to be using. Some psychoactive drugs are toxic to the developing fetus.

Quaaludes, as a powerful sedative-hypnotic psychoactive drug with its central nervous system depressant effects, may also cause damage to the developing fetus.

Early in fetal cell formation, called the pre-embryo stage, all the cells are the same. Then, about three days after the egg has been fertilized by the sperm, when the cells number about one hundred, they begin to differentiate. This means that they start to change, to become different types of cells. No one knows yet just how this happens, but some of those one hundred cells will start to divide into brain cells, some into cells in the spinal cord, some into heart, fingers, ears. They will become all the varied and specialized cells that make up the human body.[20]

Cell differentiation occurs in a specific order in the developing embryo. At first, the neural tube forms. This is the beginning of the brain and spinal cord. Soon tiny buds indicate where the differentiating cells will become hands and feet. Cells that will become organs such as the heart begin to differentiate. During the first twelve weeks of pregnancy, drugs are a serious threat to the normal development of a fetus.

Drugs taken during pregnancy that interfere with normal cell development can cause birth defects. Sedative-hypnotic drugs have been related to an increased chance of cleft palate and cleft lip in which there is a division or split in the roof of the mouth or the lip.[21] Although not proven in tests on humans, testing on mice and rats has indicated that taking quaaludes during pregnancy increases the chance of harm to the fetus.[22]

The developing fetus is at risk when the mother uses a sedative-hypnotic drug like quaaludes because the fetus is so small and its ability to metabolize drugs is not fully developed. The unmetabolized drug remains in the fetus longer and at higher levels than

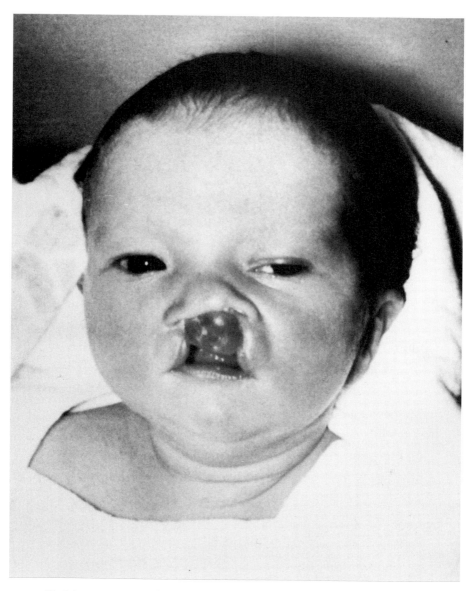

Cleft lip and cleft palate are birth defects that have been associated with the mother's use of sedative-hypnotic drugs during pregnancy. The drug interferes with normal cell development during critical periods of fetal growth.

in the mother. The drug's effects are much stronger in the fetus. They can cause the fetus's activity to be depressed, its heart rhythm to be abnormal. The drug's effects could even cause the fetus to die.[23]

The Newborn Baby, Its Mother, and Drugs

Once it has been born, a baby whose mother used drugs during her pregnancy will retain the drug's by-products in its system for an extended time—days or even weeks longer than the drugs affect the mother. The baby may be lethargic, have poor muscle tone, and have difficulty sucking (which is crucial for it to survive). Its central nervous system may be depressed.

A baby born to a drug-using mother suffers the effects of its mother's drug use and may even go through withdrawal after it has been born and no longer receives the drug. Many problems can arise when a newborn arrives with drug addiction. These babies are difficult and expensive to care for. They require specialized long-term hospital care, which can cost as much as $28,000 for withdrawal treatment. Treating and caring for a premature infant who is withdrawing from drugs and requires intensive care for months can cost as much as $135,000.[24]

The drugs a mother takes also pass into the milk her body produces. Babies who nurse from a drug-using mother will receive the drugs in their mother's milk. A nursing baby exposed to the psychoactive drugs its mother is taking may be sedated.[25]

Babies have a sequence of development. The first thing a baby learns is to communicate the state of its body and feelings to its mother or other caregiver. It does this by its behavior: how it moves its body and limbs, cries, and reacts. The mother "reads" the infant's behavior and responds appropriately. If the baby is sedated, or its behavior is distorted because it is withdrawing from drugs, it cannot communicate well. If the mother is unable or unwilling to read her infant's behavior, possibly because she is under the influence of drugs, the baby will not receive the care and nurturing it needs to thrive.[26]

The Teen Years and the Family: Conflict and Growth

The teen years are a time of physical change, social readjusting, and moral evaluation. They can also be a time of family conflict.

Teens have an emerging need for independence. Parents wish to retain authority. Teens strive to find a sense of "self" separate from the family. The family, however, often wishes the family unit to remain unchanged. Young people are also often strongly impulsive, acting on the spur of the moment. They are risk takers, dare seekers, rule testers. For the teen, all the excitement of self-identity and self-discovery, of independence, of new possibilities, may be tempered by conflict with parents and other family members.

In the adolescent years, being with friends becomes more important than being with the family. Friends' opinions and approval begin to mean more than parents' opinions. Past ways of doing things and solving problems are no longer accepted without question as they were when the teen was a small child. Moral values once accepted may be questioned, and a new, personal sense of moral values begins to develop. The family may show disappointment and anger at the teen's rejection of the family and its strongly held beliefs.

The physical changes and seesaw mood swings that accompany an adolescent's emerging sexuality can be bewildering to both teen and family. Behavior and response are less predicable as surging hormone production changes the developing adolescent's personal chemistry.

Times of change are usually disruptive. Disruption can be dangerous, or it can become an occasion to grow. The adolescent years, with the many physical, emotional, and social changes that occur in passing from childhood to adulthood, are also a time of growth.

Life inevitably has problems, and the adolescent years are an appropriate time to learn how to deal with problems. Within the family's protective environment, teens can learn to face life's painful times. With the family's support, they can practice making informed decisions and acting with ever-growing good judgment. Children who have chances to develop decision-making skills and to make critical choices within a family framework are less easily influenced by peer pressure and popular trends when they become teens. They are also less likely to become involved with drugs.

Becoming competent in conducting one's life, and eventually a job, requires self-direction and internal control. It also requires knowing how to get along with others and being able to postpone gratification. Adolescents who are encouraged to make critical choices within the family environment acquire skills for personal competence in the future.[27]

Children who have a strong sense of contributing to the family's welfare are less likely to become involved with drugs, especially when their contribution is acknowledged and considered important. Parents who acknowledge the child's role in the family's welfare and who keep lines of communication open, who themselves have decision-making and problem-solving skills, can offer informed advice and support to their children.

All families have certain common, basic areas of behavior. How a particular family operates within these areas of behavior can affect its role in the potential for drug abuse by family members. Some areas of family behavior are:

- *How does the family show and receive affection and give verbal signs of appreciation?*

- *How well do the family members hang together? How cohesive are they?*

- *What bonds exist among the members? How do they relate to each other?*

- *How well does the family communicate to identify feelings, problems, weaknesses, and strengths?*

- *What skills do they have to recognize a problem and then act to solve it?*

The family unit is the first line of defense for its children. With involved parenting, informed guidance, and support in making critical decisions, the risk that youth will repeat the mistakes of the Quaalude Culture of the 70s lessens. The family's behavior is the force that can help young children proceed to their teens, through adolescence, and into young adulthood with skills and strengths gained in the clarity of drug-free lives.

Questions for Discussion

1. Some people find out too late that they have an in-born predisposition to drug abuse. What do you think this means?

2. List five different aspects of a family's environment. Talk about ways that family members can contribute positively to each aspect of the environment.

3. Discuss why you think an older brother or sister's use of drugs influences younger siblings in their decision to try drugs.

6

How and Where to Get Help

If you suspect that you have a problem with drugs or are worried that someone you know may have one, it is very important to talk to another person about it. By telling someone else about your concern, you put into words the need for help and start the process of building a network of support and guidance.

The person you choose to talk to should be someone you believe is trustworthy and has good judgment, and with whom you feel comfortable. Some people to consider are

- *A parent, or an older brother or sister.*

- *A grandparent, uncle, aunt, an older cousin. (In drug-using families, some members may not have the objectivity to be helpful.)*

- *A good friend of the family.*

- *A good friend or the parent of a good friend.*

- *A teacher, principal, or counselor at your school.*

- *A religious leader such as a minister, priest, or rabbi. A youth ministry leader or religious education teacher.*

- *Your pediatrician or other doctor.*

- *A social worker.*

- *A neighbor you can confide in.*

- *A leader in an organization such as the Boy Scouts and Girl Scouts, 4-H, Girls Clubs and Boys Clubs of America, Big Brothers and Big Sisters.*

If you cannot think of a person you feel you can talk to, there are hot lines and helping agencies to call. Many of them are toll-free. They will point you in the appropriate direction to get help. Some of the of places you can call are:

National Youth Crisis Hotline.
(800) 448-4663.

Open twenty-four hours a day, seven days a week. Talks to the caller to assess the problem. Gives names, addresses, and telephone numbers for sources of help closest to where the caller lives. Asks the caller to call the hot line back if referred sources of help do not work out.

National Drug Information and Treatment Hotline
(800) 662-4357 (800-662-HELP)
(800) 66-AYUDA for Spanish speaking callers

Can be called from any state, Puerto Rico, and the Virgin Islands. Staffed seven days a week, twenty-four hours a day. Gives information about drug treatment options, drug treatment referrals, alcohol problems, and adolescent or family problems. Other sources of drug information and help are:

Community drug hot lines

Look in the telephone directory Yellow Pages under the Drug Abuse and Addiction heading.

Hospital chemical dependency units and help lines

Listed in telephone directories. A call to one of them puts you in touch with someone who can suggest appropriate contacts for you to make. Hospitals usually have twenty-four hour drug and alcohol information phone lines.

Drug counseling and treatment services

Listed in the Yellow Pages.

Before you start making calls, be sure to have pencil and paper at hand. The agency you call first may have other, more appropriate sources of help for you to call. You will want to write down the names and numbers as they are given to you.

Other sources of help are organizations that have youth out-reach programs or drug education and drug referrals as part of their programs. Three such organizations are the Lions Club and the Boys Club and Girls Club of America.

The governments of every state, territory, and possession of the United States has a division devoted to health and human services with drug information departments. They are listed in telephone directories under the state's name and sub-headings for the various departments. City and county governments also have mental health agencies that handle drug-related matters. Universities and some junior colleges have drug information centers and hot lines. At the end of this chapter are names, addresses, and phone numbers for other drug information and treatment sources.

Getting Help: What to Expect

Drug abuse and addiction involve many different aspects of human need, expression, and behavior. These aspects consist of a combination of biological, social, environmental, and chemical toxicity factors. Drug-abuse treatment takes all of these factors into account and can vary from one person to another and with different drugs.

The kind of drug or drugs, the combinations in which they are used, and the psychological and social conditions under which they have been taken influence the treatment program. The detoxification part of treatment for quaalude use requires medical supervision because, as a sedative-hypnotic with central nervous system depressing powers, sudden withdrawal from quaaludes can be dangerous and life-threatening.

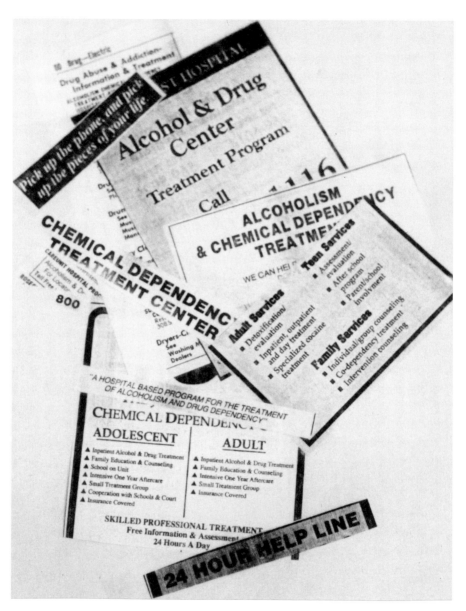

The Yellow Pages in city and town telephone directories contain sources of help for drug abuse and addiction. Listings are for hospitals and treatment centers that are open twenty-four hours and frequently have toll-free numbers.

For all drug treatment, the first step is for the user to recognize and accept that he or she does have a drug problem. It has been said that "Addiction is the only illness which requires a self diagnosis for treatment to be effective."[1]

A diagnosis of addiction can be made by tools such as the Diagnostic and Statistical Manual of Mental Disorders, which uses the pattern of drug use and length of time used, the negative effect the drug has on the user's social life and work, and symptoms of tolerance or withdrawal. Another diagnostic tool, the Selective Severity Assessment, indicates how severe the addiction is by measuring eleven physiologic signs such as pulse, temperature, and tremors.[2]

Some drug abusers also have mental illness such as depression, anxiety, and personality disorders. They are said to be *dually* diagnosed. Each disorder—the mental health part and the substance abuse part—must be treated separately. *Triple diagnosis* occurs when AIDS or AIDS-related conditions are also present in the dually diagnosed individual.[3]

Treatment for drug dependence usually involves a multipart program. Removing the drug from the system, or detoxification, works toward rebalancing the brain's neurochemistry. Other parts of a program emphasize abstinence from the drug in the short term, keeping drug-free over the long term, and learning ways to maintain a drug-free life.

A drug treatment program can include family sessions, meeting and interacting with a group of people, and learning to develop new emotions and feelings. It may suggest ways to change a lifestyle so it includes pleasantly rewarding activities that stimulate one's own endogenous drug production. The most effective treatment programs are those that are sensitive to cultural

93

differences and incorporate cultural values and experiences into their approach.

The length of time spent in a treatment program varies from person to person. Working to overcome a drug problem can be long term. It can also be expensive, although public or nonprofit programs are available for people with limited resources. The best drug treatment program is preventative: It begins when you decide that you do not want to use drugs, and it lasts throughout a drug-free lifetime.

Quaaludes proved to be a seriously addictive drug. In just a couple of weeks, the user can become physically and psychologically dependent on them. The relaxed euphoria produced by quaaludes alters judgment, perception, and inhibitions. Sudden withdrawal from large doses can interrupt respiration, cause heart rate changes, seizures, coma, and even death.

The quaalude pills sold illegally on the street today frequently contain none of the actual psychoactive ingredient methaqualone, but rather unknown quantities of drugs such as tranquilizers and antihistamines. These pills pose great risks to the user, since he or she has no idea what is being taken. Should you be presented with the opportunity to experiment with quaaludes, you know enough about this drug to be forewarned: The best way to avoid its physical, psychological, and developmental hazards is to never try it in the first place.

Questions for Discussion

1. Why do you think it is so important to talk to someone about drug problem concerns?

2. Families often become partners in a drug user's treatment program. Discuss reasons for this.

3. Put yourself in this scenario: A friend has tried quaaludes several times and has found himself or herself thinking about the drug and its effects more and more often. Your friend wonders if he or she has a potential drug problem. Describe the plan of action you would develop for your friend.

Where to Write

American Council for Drug Education
204 Monroe Street, Suite 110
Rockville, MD 20850
(301) 294-0600
(800) 488-DRUG

Families Anonymous, Inc.
P.O. Box 528
Van Nuys, CA 91408
(818) 989-7841

Narcotics Anonymous
P.O. Box 9863
Washington, D.C. 20016
(202) 399-5316

National AIDS Hotline
(800) 342-2437 in English
(800) 344-7432 in Spanish

National Clearinghouse for Alcohol & Drug Abuse Information
P.O. Box 2345
Rockville, MD 20847
(800) 729-6686

National Council on Alcoholism and Drug Dependence (NCADD)
12 West 21st Street
New York, NY 10010
(212) 206-6770
(800)622-2255

National Families in Action
2296 Henderson Mill Road
Suite 300
Atlanta, GA 30345
(770) 934-6364

National Institute on Drug Abuse (NIDA)
5600 Fishers Lane
Rockville, MD 20857
(800) 662-HELP

Phoenix House
164 West 74th Street
New York, NY 10023
(212) 595-5810

Target—Helping Students Cope with Alcohol and Drugs
P.O. Box 20626
11724 NW Plaza Circle
Kansas City, MO 64195
(816) 464-5400

Chapter Notes

Chapter 1

1. Richard Rudgley, *Essential Substances: A Cultural History of Intoxicants in Society* (New York: Kodansha America, Inc., 1994), p. 39.
2. Ibid., p. 78.
3. Telephone interview with beading expert Teri Brown, June 13, 1995.
4. Philip Nobile, "The Politics of Quaalude," *New York*, August 7, 1978, p. 66.
5. "The Deadly Downer," *Time*, March 5, 1973, p.73.
6. Nobile, p. 66.
7. Ibid.
8. Ibid.
9. Interview with Wayne Roques, Demand Reduction Coordinator, U.S. Department of Justice, Drug Enforcement Administration, Miami Field Division, May 13, 1995.
10. Mireya Navarro, "In South, Drug Abusers Turn to a Smuggled Sedative," *The New York Times*, December 9, 1995, p. 6.
11. Ibid.
12. Ibid.

Chapter 2

1. Darryl S. Inaba and William E. Cohen, *Uppers, Downers, All Arounders: Physical and Mental Effects of Psychoactive Drugs*, 2nd ed. (Ashland, Oreg.: CNS Productions, Inc., 1993), pp. 186–192.
2. Matthew Ellenhorn and Donald Barceloux, *Medical Toxicology: Diagnosis and Treatment of Human Poisoning* (New York: Elsevier, 1988), p. 596.
3. *The Merck Index*, 11th ed. (Rahway, N.J.: Merck & Co., Inc., 1989), Monograph number 5873, pp. 939–940.
4. Darryl S. Inaba, George R. Gay, John A. Newmeyer, and Craig Whitehead, "Methaqualone Abuse: Luding Out," *Journal of the American Medical Association*, June 11, 1973, p. 1505.
5. Inaba and Cohen, p. 121.

6. Joseph Carey, Ed., *Brain Facts: A Primer on the Brain and Nervous System* (Washington, D.C.: Society for Neuroscience, 1990), p. 8.

7. Paul D. Martin, *Messengers to the Brain: Our Fantastic Five Senses, Books for World Explorers* (Washington, D.C.: National Geographic Society, 1984), p. 32.

8. Charles Perry, "Unconscious Expansion: The Sopor Story," *Rolling Stone*, March 29, 1973, pp. 1, 10.

9. Interview with Dr. Earl Siegel, University of Cincinnati Drug and Poison Information Center, April 19, 1995.

10. Ellenhorn and Barceloux, p. 597.

11. Marilyn Carroll and Gary Gallo, *Quaaludes: The Quest for Oblivion* (New York: Chelsea House Publishers, 1985), p. 27.

12. Neil Henry, David T. Friendly, Vincent Coppola, and bureau reports, "The Quaalude Scam," *Newsweek*, September 28, 1981, p. 93.

13. "The Deadly Downer," *Time*, March 5, 1973, p. 74.

14. Inaba and Cohen, p. 44.

15. Carroll and Gallo, p. 64.

16. Ibid., pp. 62–63.

17. Ibid., p. 61.

18. Ibid., pp. 61, 62.

Chapter 3

1. Richard Rudgley, *Essential Substances: A Cultural History of Intoxicants in Society* (New York: Kodansha America, 1994), pp. 124–125.

2. "The Week," *National Review*, December 8, 1972, p. 1332.

3. Philip Nobile, "The Politics of Quaalude," *New York*, August 7, 1978, p. 66.

4. Author interview with "Jane," June 25, 1995.

5. Nobile, p. 66.

6. Matt Clark with Mary Hager, "All About Quaaludes," *Newsweek*, July 31, 1978, pp. 18–19.

7. Charles Perry, "Unconscious Expansion: The Sopor Story," *Rolling Stone*, March 29, 1973, pp. 8–10.

8. Jean Carper, "Deadlier Than Heroin," *Reader's Digest*, May 1982, p. 162.

9. Interview with "John," June 14, 1995.

10. Albert Goldman, "Down at the End of Lonely Street," *Life*, June 1990, pp. 98, 101.

11. Stanley Booth, "Elvis's doctor has license suspended," *Rolling Stone*, March 6, 1980, p. 23.

12. Associated Press, "Doctor loses license," *Cincinnati Enquirer*, July 7, 1995, p. A2.

13. Nobile, p. 66.

14. Bob Woodward, *Wired: The Short Life and Fast Times of John Belushi* (New York: Simon and Schuster, 1984), pp. 105, 256, 338.

15. Ibid., p. 65.

16. Peter J. Ognibene, "There's Gold In Them There Pills," *The New Republic*, April 21, 1973, p. 14.

17. Matthew Ellenhorn and Donald Barceloux, *Medical Toxicology: Diagnosis and Treatment of Human Poisoning* (New York: Elsevier, 1988), p. 596.

18. Ognibene, p. 14.

19. Nobile, p. 69.

20. Perry, p. 10.

21. Nobile, p. 69.

22. Perry, p. 8.

23. Ognibene, p. 14.

24. Carper, p. 161.

25. Frederick Tasker, "You Might Call It a Case of Arrested Arrests," *Miami Herald*, December 7, 1982, p. 1B.

26. Darryl S. Inaba, George R. Gay, John A. Newmeyer, and Craig Whitehead, "Methaqualone Abuse: Luding Out," *Journal of the American Medical Association*, June 11, 1973, p. 1505.

27. Perry, p. 8.

28. "Thumbs Down on Downers," *Current Health* 2, April 1985, p. 17.

29. Perry, p. 8.

30. Matthew Ellenhorn and Donald Barceloux, *Medical Toxicology: Diagnosis and Treatment of Human Poisoning* (New York: Elsevier, 1988), p. 596.

31. Inaba et al., p. 1508.

32. "Latest Drug Danger: Another 'Relaxer,'" *U.S. News and World Report*, April 23, 1973, p. 60.

33. Philip Nobile, "Quaaludes' Abuse Creates Subtle Dangers: Peril Around President?," *Science Digest*, December 1978, p. 54.

34. Philip Nobile, "The Politics of Quaalude," *New York*, August 7, 1978, p. 66.

35. Carper, p. 166.

36. Ognibene, p. 31.

37. Peter Slevin and Philip Ward, "Speedboat Racing Champion Gets 16 Years in Narcotics Smuggling," *Miami Herald*, April 18, 1987, p. 1B.

38. "Pepitone Begins Jail Term," *Miami Herald*, May 17, 1988, p. 2C.

39. Peter Slevin and Philip Ward, "DEA Agents' Drug Sweep Nets 20 Men," *Miami Herald*, July 22, 1983, p. 1A.

40. Al Messerschmidt, "Halt Flow of Drug Money, State Urged," *Miami Herald*, August 10, 1983, p. 1D.

41. Interview with "Jane," June 25, 1995.

42. Inaba et al, p. 1507.

43. *Drugs of Abuse*, 1989 Ed., U.S. Department of Justice, Drug Enforcement Administration (Washington, D.C.: U.S. Government Printing Office, 1989), p. 9.

44. Interview with Wayne Roques, Demand Reduction Division, Drug Enforcement Agency, Miami, Florida, May 1, 1995.

45. Mireya Navarro, "In South, Drug Abusers Turn to a Smuggled Sedative," *The New York Times*, December 9, 1995, p. 6.

46. Ibid.

47. Interview with Wayne Roques, May 1, 1995.

48. Navarro, p. 6.

49. Darryl S. Inaba and William E. Cohen, *Uppers, Downers, All Arounders: Physical and Mental Effects of Psychoactive Drugs*, 2nd Ed. (Ashland, Oreg.: CNS Productions, 1993), p. 197.

Chapter 4

1. Andrew Weil and Winifred Rosen, *From Chocolate to Morphine: Everything You Need to Know About Mind-Altering Drugs*, revised and updated (Boston: Houghton Mifflin Company, 1993), p. 25.

2. Jack M. Gorman, M.D., *The Essential Guide to Psychiatric Drugs*, rev. ed. (New York: St. Martin's Press, 1995), p. 260.

3. Darryl S. Inaba and William E. Cohen, *Uppers, Downers, All Arounders: Physical and Mental Effects of Psychoactive Drugs*, 2nd ed. (Ashland, Oreg.: CNS Productions, Inc., 1993), p. 292.

4. Philip Nobile, "Politics of Quaalude," *New York*, August 7, 1978, p. 66.

5. "The Deadly Downer," *Time*, March 5, 1973, p. 73.

6. Darryl S. Inaba, George R. Gay, John A. Newmeyer, and Craig Whitehead, "Methaqualone Abuse: Luding Out," *Journal of the American Medical Association*, June 11, 1973, p. 1505.

7. Inaba and Cohen, p. 289.

8. Ibid., p. 269.

9. John W. Spencer, John J. Boren, *Residual Effects of Abused Drugs on Behavior*, Research Monograph Series, Monograph 101, (Rockville, Md.: National Institute on Drug Abuse, 1990), p. 72.

10. Interview with "Jane," June 25, 1995.

11. *Clinical Pharmacy and Therapeutics*, 4th ed. (Baltimore: Williams and Wilkins, 1988), p. 946.

12. Bob Woodward, *Wired: The Short Life and Fast Times of John Belushi*, hard cover, original edition, (New York: Simon and Schuster, 1984), p. 417.

Chapter 5

1. Darryl S. Inaba and William E. Cohen, *Uppers, Downers, All Arounders: Physical and Mental Effects of Psychoactive Drugs* (Ashland, Oreg.: CNS Productions, 1993), p. 139.

2. Roy W. Pickens and Dace S. Svikis, eds., Biological Vulnerability to Drug Abuse, NIDA Research Monograph Series, Monograph 89 (Rockville, Md.: National Institute on Drug Abuse, 1988), pp. v, 1, 2.

3. *Prevention in Action: 1991 Exemplary Alcohol and Other Drug Prevention Programs* (Rockville, Md.: Office for Substance Abuse Prevention, 1991), p. 20.

4. Inaba and Cohen, p. 45.

5. Pickens and Svikis, pp. 3–4.

6. James N. Butcher, "Personality Factors In Drug Addiction," *Biological Vulnerability to Drug Abuse*, NIDA Research Monograph Series, Monograph 89 (Rockville, Md.: National Institute on Drug Abuse, 1988), pp. 87–88.

7. Pickens and Svikis, p. 3.

8. Jean Carper, "Deadlier Than Heroin," *Reader's Digest*, May 1982, p. 162.

9. Inaba and Cohen, p. 115.

10. Stephen E. Garner, Patricia F. Green, and Carol Marcus, eds. *Signs of Effectiveness II. Preventing Alcohol, Tobacco, and Other Drug Use: A Risk Factor/Resiliency-Based Approach*, DHHS Publication No. (SAM) 94-2098, (Rockville, Md.: Center for Substance Abuse Prevention, 1994), p. 10.

11. Mark S. Gold, *The Good News About Drugs and Alcohol: Curing, Treating and Preventing Substance Abuse in the New Age of Biopsychiatry* (New York: Villard Books, 1991), p. 40.

12. "Prevention Research," RP 0780, reprinted from *The Third Triennial Report to Congress from the Secretary*, Publication No. (ADM) 91-1704, Department of Health and Human Services, Rockville, Md., 1991, p. 35.

13. Gold, p. 37.

14. Garner et. al., p. 10.

15. Carper, p. 162.

16. Gold, p. 14.

17. Inaba and Cohen, p. 336.

18. Garner et al., p. 10

19. *Pregnancy and Exposure to Alcohol and Other Drug Use*, CSAP Technical Reports Series, Technical Report 7 (Rockville, Md.: Center for Substance Abuse Prevention, 1993), p. 2.

20. Joel L. Swerdlow, "Quiet Miracles of the Brain," *National Geographic*, June 1995, pp. 9–10.

21. *Pregnancy*, p. 24.

22. Information summarized from database for *Reproductive Toxicity Review*, courtesy of the Genetics Department, Children's Hospital Medical Center, Cincinnati, OH.

23. *Pregnancy*, p. 24.

24. Ibid, pp. 24, 105.

25. Ewart A. Swinyard, "Sedatives and Hypnotics," *Remington's Pharmaceutical Sciences*, 18th ed. (Easton, Penna: Mack Publishing Co., 1990), p. 3–4.

26. *Identifying the Needs of Drug-Affected Children: Public Policy Issues*, OSAP Prevention Monograph Series, Monograph 11, (Rockville, Md.: Office for Substance Abuse Prevention, 1992), pp. 3–4.

27. Diana Baumrind, "Familial Antecedents of Adolescent Drug Use: A Developmental Perspective," *Etiology of Drug Abuse: Implications for Prevention*, NIDA Research Monograph Series, Monograph 56 (Rockville, Md.: National Institute on Drug Abuse, 1985), pp. 13–37.

Chapter 6

1. Darryl S. Inaba and William E. Cohen, *Uppers, Downers, All Arounders: Physical and Mental Effects of Psychoactive Drugs.* 2nd ed. (Ashland, Oreg.: CNS Productions, 1993), p. 308.

2. Ibid., p. 307.

3. Ibid., p. 329.

Glossary

acid—The street name for LSD (lysergic acid diethylamide).

addiction—An uncontrollable urge to use a drug or other substance.

amphetamines—Powerful synthetic stimulant drugs.

apnea—The absence or suspension of breathing.

ataxia—The loss or lack of muscle coordination.

axon—A nerve fiber extending from one neuron that passes messages to other neurons.

biochemistry—The chemical reactions that occur in living organisms.

blood-brain barrier—Specialized cells lining the blood vessels that enter the brain. They prevent harmful substances from reaching the brain.

central nervous system—The brain and spinal cord.

chromosomes—Part of the cell nucleus that contains the genes that are responsible for transmitting hereditary traits.

coma—A state of deep unconsciousness.

controlled substance—A drug whose manufacture, use, and possession are controlled by federal law.

convulsion—A series of intense, involuntary muscular contractions.

counterfeit drugs—Illegally manufactured tablets and capsules identical in appearance to legally made tablets and capsules.

cross-tolerance—When tolerance to one drug makes the user tolerant to other similar drugs also.

DNA—Deoxyribonucleic acid, a large molecule that carries genetic information.

depressant—A drug that reduces functioning of the central nervous system.

differentiate—To develop into specialized cells or tissues.

disinhibiting effect—To reduce or lower restraints on behavior.

downer—A drug that depresses the central nervous system.

drug—A substance that when taken into the body by any means produces changes in physical or mental function.

drug abuse—Use of psychoactive drugs to the point where the user's health, employment, or social functioning are affected.

dually diagnosed—Having both drug abuse problems and psychiatric illness.

endogenous—Produced from within the body.

endorphins—The body's own drugs—made by the body, within the body.

environment—The total physical, social, and cultural circumstances surrounding a person.

enzymes—Proteins manufactured by the body which speed up biochemical reactions.

euphoria—A feeling of well-being or happiness.

exogenous—Derived from outside the body.

fetus—An unborn developing baby.

gastrointestinal—Pertaining to the stomach and intestines.

genes—The parts of DNA that direct the production of specific proteins that determine hereditary traits.

hallucinogen—A substance that causes the user to experience objects, events, or sensations that do not exist in reality.

hemorrhage—Heavy bleeding.

hormone—A biochemical made in one organ that stimulates another organ to function.

hypnotic effect—Causing sleep.

inhalant—A substance whose vapors are breathed into the lungs for its drug-like effect.

inhibitions—Restraints on personal actions or expressions.

insomnia—The inability to sleep over a prolonged period of time.

lateral nystagmus—A "bouncing" movement of the eyes associated with quaalude use.

lethal dose—The amount of a drug which causes death.

luding out—Combining quaaludes with alcohol for a more pronounced effect.

metabolism—The process by which the body breaks down complex molecules into simpler molecules in order to use them or get rid of them.

metabolite—A broken-down product of metabolism.

methaqualone—The chemical name for quaaludes.

mind-altering substance—Any substance which causes changes in the brain's function.

necrotizing cystitis—A disease of the bladder caused by impurities left in street drugs.

neural tube—The earliest cells in the fetal development of the brain and spinal cord.

neuron—A nerve cell.

neurotransmitters—biochemical messengers that enable nerve cells to communicate with each other and with other cells.

neutralize—To break down into simpler or less harmful products.

overdose—The result of taking more of a drug than needed for the desired effect.

paresthesia—Tingling of parts of the body such as lips, tongue, or fingers.

physical dependence—The body's adaptation to a drug so that when the drug is absent, withdrawal symptoms occur.

placenta—The organ that develops during pregnancy to transfer nourishment and oxygen from the mother to the fetus.

placental barrier—Cells in the placenta that prevent toxic substances from passing from the mother's blood to the fetus.

psychedelic—Causing distorted perceptions.

psychoactive—Having an effect on brain function.

psychological dependence—Craving a drug to feel good and feeling bad when deprived of the drug,

Rohypnol^{TM}—Trade name for flunitrazapam, a powerful sedative drug with addicting properties which is illegal in the United States.

schedule of drugs—Federally-determined categories of substances and the limitations, prohibitions, and penalties placed on their manufacture, use, and possession.

sedative effect—A calming, relaxing effect.

seizure—A sudden and involuntary outburst of action or emotion.

side effects—Unintended and unexpected effects from use of a drug.

synapse—A space between nerve endings.

synergism—When two drugs acting together produce an effect that is greater than their individual effects added together.

synthetic drugs—Drugs that are artificially made by combining chemicals.

tolerance—Adaptation to a drug so that larger and larger amounts are needed to give the original effect.

trafficking—Trading or dealing in illegal drugs.

triple diagnosis—Being drug dependent, having psychiatric illness, and having AIDS.

upper—A stimulant drug.

uterus—The organ in a woman's body that holds the fetus during its development.

withdrawal—The effects experienced by the body and the brain when drug use is stopped.

Further Reading

Berger, Gilda. *Drug Abuse: The Impact on Society.* New York: Franklin Watts, 1988.

——. *Making Up Your Mind About Drugs.* New York: E.P. Dutton, 1988.

Carroll, Marilyn, and Gary Gallo. *Quaaludes: The Quest for Oblivion.* Updated version. New York: Chelsea House Publishers, 1992.

Fradin, Dennis. *Drug Abuse.* Chicago: Children's Press, 1988.

Hawley, Richard. *Drugs and Society.* New York: Walker and Company, 1992.

Hughes, Barbara. *Drug-related Diseases.* New York, Franklin Watts, 1987.

Hyde, Margaret. *Know About Drugs.* 4th ed. New York: Walker and Company, 1996.

——. *Mind Drugs.* 5th ed. New York: Dodd, Mead, and Company, 1986.

Inaba, Darryl S. and William E. Cohen. *Uppers, Downers, All Arounders: Physical and Mental Effects of Psychoactive Drugs.* 2nd ed. Ashland, Oreg.: CNS Productions, 1993.

Irwin, Samuel. *Drugs of Abuse: An Introduction to Their Actions and Potential Hazards.* Tempe, Ariz.: D.I.N Publications, 1995.

Kronenwetter, Michael. *Drugs in America: The Users, The Suppliers, the War on Drugs.* New York: Julian Messner, 1990.

Landau, Elaine. *Hooked.* Brookfield, Conn.: Millbrook Press, 1995.

Madison, Arnold. *Drugs and You.* Rev. ed. Englewood Cliffs, N.J.: Julian Messner, 1990.

McMillan, Daniel. *Winning the Battle Against Drugs: Rehabilitation Programs:* New York: Franklin Watts, 1991.

Navarra, John. *Drugs and Man.* Garden City, New York: Doubleday, 1973.

Seixas, Judith. *Living With a Parent Who Takes Drugs.* New York: Beech Tree Books, 1991.

Sonder, Ben. *The Babies of Drug-Taking Parents.* New York: Franklin Watts, 1994.

Ward, Brian R. *Drugs and Drug Abuse.* New York: Franklin Watts, 1987.

Weil, Andrew, and Winifred Rosen. *From Chocolate to Morphine: Everything You Need to Know About Mind-Altering Drugs.* Revised and updated. New York: Houghton Mifflin, 1993.

Index

in seeking help, 88
competence
  personal, 85
  social, 62
controlled substances
  quaaludes, 49
  restrictions on, 10
  Rohypnol, 15
convulsions, 11

D
death, 32
  from overdose, 11, 50
decision-making skills, 85
dependence, 66, 74
depression, 9, 59
  mental disorders, 93
  sleeping problems, 60
desired mental effect, 12
  tolerance, 30
detoxification
  monitoring, 36
  process, 36
  rebalancing brain chemistry, 93
  sedative-hypnotic drugs, 91
development
  and growth, 58
  sequence in babies, 83
diagnosis of addiction, 93
differentiation
  fetal cell formation, 81
digestion, 57
DNA, 72
downers, 18, 26
drug abuse
  diagnosis of addiction, 93
  help for, 79, 90, 91
  tendency toward, 73
drug cycles, 54
drug dealing, 11
drug effects, 59
  on fetus, 83
  set and setting, 59
Drug Enforcement Agency, 12, 54
drug manufacturing, 28
  illegal labs, 11
drug neutralization, 33

drug use
  age of first use, 77
  in eighth graders, 55
dual diagnosis, 93

E
egg cell, 72
emergency room visits, 11, 12
endogenous drugs, 68, 93
  personal high, 69
  production of, 69
endorphins, 68
environment
  family, 75, 78
  setting, 59
enzymes, 73
  drug neutralizing, 33
ethnic groups
  drug metabolism differences, 74
euphoria, 26, 69, 94
exogenous drugs, 68, 70
expanded consciousness, 66
experimentation, 66, 74, 78

F
family
  attitudes about drug use, 75
  cohesiveness, 79
  instability, 79
  relationships, 40
fetus
  activity of, 83
  brain development, 81
  cell differentiation, 81
  drug effects on, 81

G
gastrointestinal disturbance, 28
genetic inheritance, 72
  tendency toward drug use, 74
Girls Club of America, 91

H
heart rate, 18, 20, 94
help, 88-91
hemorrhage
  intestinal, 28

and oxygen supply, 80
and premature labor, 80
drug effects on, 81
sedative-hypnotic drug effects on, 79
prescriptions, 10
sedative-hypnotic drugs, 77
"script" doctors, 46
Presley, Elvis, 43, 44
Prinze, Freddie, 44
problem-solving, 77
proteins, 57, 72
psychedelics, 18
psychoactive drugs,
depressants, 18
methaqualone, 20
synthetic, 8
toxicity to fetus, 81
purity of drugs, 11

Q
"Quaalude Alley," 11
"Quaalude Culture," 40, 78
quaaludes
and alcohol, 11
and gender, 58
and lowered inhibitions, 65
and pain threshold, 27
reclassification, 49
recreational use, 46
sedative-hypnotic effects, 9, 20
storage in body, 58
strength of, 10
synergism, 34
withdrawal, 35-37

R
recreational drugs, 10, 40, 46
respiratory failure, 35
responsibility, 62
risk
and teens, 84
factors in family, 78
to fetus, 81
Rohypnol, 15-16
addiction, 15
and alcohol, 16, 54

duration of effects, 15, 54
street names for, 54
Rolling Stone magazine, 26

S
Schedule I drugs, 14, 50, 53
Schedule II drugs, 12, 50
"script" doctor, 46
Scythian, 6
secret labs, 11
sedative effect
of quaaludes, 20
of Rohypnol, 15
sedative-hypnotic drugs, 9
and cross tolerance, 32
and pregnancy, 79
Selective Severity Assessment, 93
self esteem, 59, 74, 78, 79
sexual assault, 65
sexual performance, 63
sexuality, 58, 85
sexually transmitted diseases, 65
society
and attitudes toward drugs, 50
and recreational drugs, 40
sperm cells, 72
stomach, 28, 35
suicide, 49, 50, 51 59, 74
Sumerians, 5
synthetic drugs, 8

T
taxiing, 27
tolerance, 30-32
tranquilizers, 22, 39
triple diagnosis, 93

V
Valium, 22, 39

W
wall banger, 27
Williams, Robin, 70
withdrawal, 29, 35-37
and newborns, 83
during pregnancy, 80
treatment programs, 93–94